Volume 1 of the Trilogy

MY FATHER *the* GAMEKEEPER

Early Years

Anne M. White

authorHOUSE®

AuthorHouse™ UK Ltd.
500 Avebury Boulevard
Central Milton Keynes, MK9 2BE
www.authorhouse.co.uk
Phone: 08001974150

© 2009 Anne M. White. All rights reserved.

No part of this book may be reproduced, stored in a retrieval system, or transmitted by any means without the written permission of the author.

First published by AuthorHouse 7/28/2009

ISBN: 978-1-4490-1098-0 (sc)

This book is printed on acid-free paper.

THIS BOOK IS LOVINGLY DEDICATED
TO MY FATHER AND TO MY WONDERFUL
MOTHER FOR PUTTING UP WITH HIM
FOR SO MANY YEARS

Acknowledgements

I would like to give a big thanks to those who have supported me throughout the last few years. They know who they are. Thank you for your patience and understanding. I wouldn't have got this far without you.

On visits to their home I thank my mother for her patience (having heard it all before). Thanks dad for your patience too and making time for me to ask so many questions and giving me so much insight into your life, most of which I never knew or understood during my childhood. Now I feel I really know you dad.

I would also like to give a special thanks to my one and only daughter. She has painstakingly repaired some of the old photographs along the way to be used in my books.

It has certainly been an enjoyable learning curve for all of us.

Contents

Preface	1
Natures Playground	5
They Thought They Were Otters	13
Out On A Limb	22
Absent Without Leave	27
Farm Education	31
Beast Of The Fields	35
Giving A Fly A Parting	39
Countryside Connoisseurs	44
Birds In The Bedroom	47
Spitfires And Harvests	51
Exercising Cats And Dogs	61
The Boys Menagerie	65
The Lodger Experience	73
Little Scavengers	80
Burning Rubber	86
Back On The Farm	92
Gamekeeper At Last	100
Absence Makes The Heart Grow Fonder	108

And Now There Were Two	124
Army Years	133
Homesickness	145
The Gypsy Caravan	160
Bonafide Vermin Officer	173
All In A Days Work	177
Before The Judge And Off With His Thumb	183
The Move To Hertfordshire	187
Gamekeeper At Work	192
Foxes And Hens	202
Aquaintance With Poachers	209
Free As A Bird	224
It's A Dangerous Life	229
Keen To Move On	241
Christmas Spirit	261

PREFACE

My father George White has for many years wanted to write his life story but felt he could not achieve this on his own.

A number of people with writing abilities including journalists have tried over the years to take down some of his stories but he was not pleased with the results as they were too clinical in their approach.

I took along a friend one day to visit him, who was very interested in his work as a gamekeeper and the amusing tales he told of his wonderful life. My father readily showed him some of his scrap books which contained snapshots and memorabilia of his clay shooting career, whilst recounting some amusing tales of his life.

For me it was no surprise as I took it all for granted since I had grown up with it all and been in that environment, little realising how little the general public knew about a gamekeepers work and the competitive sport of clay pigeon shooting.

It was from this moment that it dawned on me to attempt to write down some of my fathers' life as I had empathy for him and the subject.

My father has achieved so much in his shooting career and met with many well known personalities, like royalty and famous movie stars, during the course of his work as a game keeper, that I felt it needed to be recorded for him in a book so that all could read it.

Many people have been influenced by him over the years and since early childhood became a born leader to many, not only at work but out in the public gaze when attending clay shoots. He had a large following from around the country as he went to organised clay shoots all over and was often featured in the Shooting Times and Country Magazine especially throughout the sixties and seventies. People would turn up to watch him in action and follow his progress.

My mother had the thankless task of polishing all the many hundreds of cups and trophies he won over the years and thankfully started to keep a few of his photographs and letters in a scrap book at the height of his career. She has supported him throughout his working life on the estates and gave him encouragement and often her own housekeeping money to enter the clay shoots all on the promise that if he went round again that he could get an even higher score and win the cash prize. This meant she would get her money back with some interest and it was achieved most times.

In his work as a gamekeeper my father has met some wonderful characters and been in some very amusing incidents which he loves to share with his friends and family. Many will recognise some of the tales I retell in these chapters and smile once again over them. There are still more to be recorded.

It is my fathers wish to include some of the people who have become a part of his life's journey and who were and still are important to him.

Many people have misconceptions about what a keeper's job entails and I would like to put the record straight where I can in my writing, along with showing how in these modern times that a gamekeeper is the custodian of the countryside and the environment he lives and works.

In this first part of the trilogy, "The Early Years" rules were indeed different and very few practices were illegal for the keeper as they are today.

I wish to point out that it was during the fifties that methods of capturing wildlife like using the Gin traps, poisons and gasses so far used in a gamekeepers work were banned from use. At about the same time protection for the wildlife became a priority as some species declined in numbers and the game keepers had to abide by the laws too and suffer the same consequences if caught breaking these laws. The gamekeepers take note and look after and protect these species now, whatever they are rather than shooting or destroying them as has been done in the past.

Although things are far from ideal today, I will also attempt to show just how far we have come, during the span of my father's lifetime, in respecting and protecting our countryside and indeed our heritage, with all its beautiful wild life, flora and fauna.

It has been a huge task to record all the information I have gained doing my research and I feel I have been on a journey of discovery. Even I at the start thought I knew it all but have been proved very wrong.

There's more to my father than is first seen and he has imparted to me some very deep felt thoughts and emotions about his work and life. Hopefully I will convey this in my writing which is from the heart.

What started for me as a hobby a couple of hours a day after I finished work of an afternoon, soon became much more serious. I had to learn to use a computer and all the paraphernalia needed to write a book and record all my interviews with my father. This has so far been quite a challenge for me.

I am more used to throwing a few ingredients together to make pies, stews, puddings and cakes than attempting to write a trilogy of books as I am a cook in a local residential home for the elderly. Over the years I have always said there is no room or use for a computer in the kitchen so never gave it much credit until now where it has become one of my best friends.

Because I have so much information which is growing weekly I decided to cover all I can and split my fathers' life into parts coming to the conclusion of having a trilogy of books. The first to be called "My Father the Gamekeeper, Early years," in which I retell from the start of his humble beginnings in the *"University of Life"* in the Norfolk countryside which he found himself. Carrying on with the next phase "My Father the Gamekeeper, Top Gun" which encompasses his shooting career during which he not only shot for England, but for Great Britain also, bringing home medals from international shoots whilst still working full time as a head keeper on a large private estate. "My father the Gamekeeper, Later Years." will show how the work of a keeper has moved on into this present time. Throughout my writing I hope to impart his love for the countryside and humour as he recounts some of his high spots in daily life in the countryside.

NATURES PLAYGROUND

He was born at the age of two, or so he told me! Actually it was July the 10th 1931, and George Walter White was born as an earthquake rattled the cups on the shelves and jiggled the pictures around on the walls of the bedroom in the large thatched cottage at Salhouse, in the county of Norfolk, England. It seems he was destined to cause a bit of a stir and to make his mark in this life. After all, the Earth moved with a shudder as his Mother pushed him out into the world.

His mothers' maiden name is Doris Ethel Edna Irene London. She was a country girl, the daughter of a local farmer to the same village my dad was born.

He is the eldest of five boys and has one older sister, Rene, and the brothers were named John, Edward (Nida), Herbert (Hado) and William, (Willy) in order of age.

His father was also called George, George Herbert White, and he worked on the local estates and farms in the area, mainly as a herdsman but at whatever job he could find. He would help out on the rearing fields with the game keepers on the local estates in the early spring and summer, whenever he could, and sometimes worked with horses or the cows on the farms.

Dads' earliest memory, he thinks, must have been when he was about two years old, out with his Father and uncle in the woods. He said it would have been May, as it was warm and there were bluebells in the woods they walked through. He was walking beside his father when a hen pheasant flapped around just in front of him, almost under his feet. He had nearly walked onto a nest that contained eight tiny, fluffy, pearly white chicks which had just hatched out. His father and uncle scooped them up to put into their sack bags which hung across on their shoulder and took them to put under a broody bantam hen they had at home, leaving the hen pheasant to hopefully lay again out in the woods.

His Father told him the chicks were his and that he was to help look after them. Five of the eight chicks survived over the following weeks and this was to be dads' first rearing success.

He recalls it was after this time they took him with them more regularly. They must have seen he had a feel for what they were about and of his natural interest in the wildlife that surrounded them.

Life in Norfolk at this time was absolutely idyllic for growing children, at least three miles from the nearest small town and surrounded by fields and woodlands, interspersed with waterways and dykes. It was a mass of thriving, wonderful, diverse wildlife.

Excitedly my father went into great detail in describing his playground, the beautiful English countryside of the 30's which he so proudly remembers and describes;

There were otters aplenty along the riverbanks and the waterways, with swallowtail butterflies amongst others in abundance in the swathes of colourful wild flowers that seemed to grow everywhere along the sides of the farm tracks and in the meadows. There were poppies and ox-eye daisies along with cornflowers and buttercups and red campions in abundance. Foxgloves sprang up in huge patches if left unchecked; grabbing a space wherever they could in the rougher grounds and along the ditches near the farm buildings. In the spring the woods were full of bluebells and anemones and patches of wild orchids, which were left to grow as they liked.

There were plenty of red squirrels around in the woodlands and badgers pottering around on the higher ground.

Down along the waters edges were the coypus who were like huge ugly rats with big yellow teeth a couple of inches long, having a short tail as thick as your wrist. They weighed anything between ten to fifteen pounds and were as big as an otter, probably standing a foot high and could be seen gnawing on the sugar beets on the edges of the fields right up to the waters edges.

They lived in holes along the banks, diving in and under if they saw you coming along. They would make tunnels from beneath the water level and dive under coming up through the tunnels, already having made an entrance up into the beet fields where they ate their weight in beet. The coypus would crawl along on their bellies most of the time. If you went out quietly of a late afternoon you could see the coypus in rows, the sun shining on all the humpbacks along the beet fields. When you looked at them like this it was difficult to tell if they were otters but as soon as they moved you could tell because an otter would lope up and down in a fluid movement, unlike the coypus who pulled themselves along on their bellies. They bred very quickly and must have been introduced by the Americans from the airbase close by as they were not natural inhabitants of this country but bred well and had plenty of food and a good environment to live in. They were often caught in the Gin traps the locals used in those days and their furs were well sought after by the furriers as it was soft, thick and sleek.

Walking along near the water, you could easily spot kingfishers flashing past, flying up and down the sandy banks amongst the brambles of the dykes and rivers along with sand martins. Marsh and hen harriers could always be spotted flying overhead. The place was teeming with wildlife on the flats, and amongst the reeds, dykes and ditches. There was a plentiful supply of coarse fish, pike, bream, perch and eels in all the clean waters. The marshlands and countryside were full of pheasant, ducks and partridges amongst many other species, along with the waterfowl. There were so many water hens and coots about; the keepers would have coot shoots by taking out a boat each to round them up.

Alder trees grew alongside the banks of the waterways along with oaks and fully mature elm trees unaffected as yet by Dutch elm disease.

Along in the fields hardy crops were growing like the thick marrow stemmed kale which was up to three inches thick and up to six feet high. There were also potatoes and swedes, sugar beets and turnips. He recalls the long piles of potatoes which they called hales alongside the edges of the field at harvest times. The potatoes were covered in straw, and then packed in soil for storage, leaving a few holes which were only filled with straw to allow them to breathe and keep fresh, stopping them from rotting. These hales would be broken open by the farmers maybe months later to sell them on.

There were no delicate crops planted in the fields

because the rabbits would eat them as they came through. This was pre-myxamatosis days and there were literally thousands of rabbits about in the fields and hedgerows, they were everywhere you looked.

This was ideal soil for the game birds as it supported a richness of flora and fauna for the wildlife which allowed the birds a plentiful supply of food and cover naturally. This was a time before the pesticides were introduced. The water was so clean you could drink it. All natural plants and wildlife were free to express themselves and grow as God intended. This beautiful natural environment supported all the inhabitants of its time.

My dad grew up and came out into this glorious scene of life every day, playing in the fields and waterways around his home with his brothers and sister. He watched all around him with wonder and awe. He says there was so much to see and enjoy, he can never remember it raining and if it did it must have done at night, because it never stopped him going out into the fields, ever. To him, the World outside never existed and those years were just one long burst of summer. He was never bored, having such a large and fantastic playground right outside his home and having his brothers and his five cousins who lived locally.

His cousins, all boys, being a little older, were born to his mothers' sister. He said his cousins taught him and his brothers a thing or two out in the countryside.

The older boys would take them out to explore the local area and of course watch all the natural inhabitants that surrounded them. They got to know the local woodlands and all the sights for nests, the names of the species and their natural habitats.

The soils in Norfolk were very good and light, perfect for all the wildlife, but especially the game birds. At the end of a shooting season in Norfolk there would be more game birds around, than there would be at the beginning of the season in the rest of the country.

Dad can't remember at what age he was first given a catapult by his granddad but he reckons it must have been about two. It was as soon as he could hold one and pull it back at full stretch. He just seems to remember he might well have been born with one already attached.

As he grew he soon found he could put the catapult to good use and took home a rabbit for the cooking pot regularly at a very early age. His mother would make the most wonderful rabbit stew with dumplings, which she boiled in a large pot over the huge black grate of the farmhouse stove that was set back into the wall of the spacious kitchen.

He and his brothers also had to go and collect the wood daily for the fires in the house, from amongst the hedgerows. This was usually hawthorn, and they would come back with the old pram piled high, from "stubbing" as they called it. He remembers his youngest baby brother would sometimes still be in the pram when it was decided life would be easier if they took it with them to carry the load back. He says that occasionally they would all hear a baby's crying like a meowing kitten from underneath the load as they all pushed the heavily laden pram on their way back home. They knew that somewhere underneath all the wood if they could hear him cry, their baby brother was fine and unharmed. He says it was one of those old deep-bottomed prams and you could get a lot of wood in it along with the baby way down deep inside.

He can still smell the rabbit stew cooking even today, and as for the flavour, it was unbeatable. His mother tried other dishes, but it wasn't such good stuff, as he remembers. Rabbit stew was her speciality and he and his family enjoyed it so much, they got it most days. There were always so many rabbits about for the cooking pot and it was dads' job as a boy to pick them off as they were needed. This was something he improved upon daily. He says he would sometimes use a stick to get a rabbit for their tea. He would be able to creep up on a rabbit in those days where they hid in the long tufts of marron grasses which grew in this part of the world. The grasses grew out up to two feet wide and about the same in height and the wild rabbits would hide beneath them. He would creep up on them from behind the huge tufts of grass with his stick at the ready and poised. He said he had to be very quiet and very quick in order to get one in this way.

His mother must have put the rabbits in the huge bucket-like pot over the fire along with some onions and flour probably not long after their breakfast as it was falling off the bone by teatime. She would also put in some swede and turnips if she had some but it was all melted down by the time it was served up. He said on some occasions his mum would boil up some onions in water on their own and serve them up along with the rabbit stew. You can imagine the effects on their stomach later on at night as they went to bed. The boys would have competitions under the blanket on who had the foulest smell and the loudest emissions. He said they stank like polecats for a week after, but he does remember it all tasted very good no matter what the consequences. At least it wasn't a problem for just one of them as they had all eaten the same food which had the same common effects on their stomachs.

When his mother did cook other meat, which occasionally his father came by, she would try to cook it in the same manner without too much success. She boiled everything. He remembers his father once brought home a huge hunk of meat the size of his head, just for a change of menu. His Mother put it into the pot over the fire, whole, as usual, to boil up. At teatime that evening his father was given his piece of what turned out to be horsemeat, and he pulled a face at its toughness, unable to cut it, and sent it flying across the table and on to the floor. Dad told me he would always be careful around his Father as he was known to have a bit of a temper and when he flew, he flew. He also knew his Mother was not the best of cooks and that her speciality dish would always be rabbit stew and huge dumplings and not much else, but boy did it taste good. They didn't know any different at the time, and it kept them all fed.

It was years later when he went for his first job away from home that he discovered other people ate a varied diet and rarely did it consist of rabbit.

His brother John had inherited their fathers' temper and was just as feisty as he, which takes him back to memories of early schooldays.

THEY THOUGHT THEY WERE OTTERS

He and his brothers and sister were sent to the school across the fields a couple of miles away, but they never wanted to go and would all look to find some excuse not to if they could. They had a number of ways of getting out of it should the need arise and had become more inventive as they grew up and if they could all get out of it they would, at the drop of a hat. They could all find so much more interesting things to do with their time. If they got stuck for an excuse they would all go out, quite purposely, he told me, to find a huge puddle of water and get their feet wet. They would have set out normally as if to go to school and then turn back knowing their mother would not send them to sit all day in the classroom with sodden shoes on. Their mother was a bit of a soft touch and they all knew it.

Dad remembers his head teacher Edna Ives at Salhouse School, because she was some sort of relation of his. He fondly remembers that most of the boys at school were in love with her and she was a well turned out, good-looking young woman.

His teacher, Mrs Green was a former London teacher who at that time also bought in evacuees to keep them safe from the bombing in London. They had another teacher called Polly Webster as well at the school.

An awful thing happened to dads' little brother John, at school. Mrs Green had been allotted as their teacher and she regularly picked on John right from the start. He had such an awful temper for a seven year old. The teacher should have known better but she somehow goaded him until one day he got up and flew at her as she was warming her backside against the coal fire in the classroom.

He hit and pummelled her in the belly, shouting at her all the while. She was shouting at him to stop as all the kids got out of their seats to congregate behind him, egging him on. Dad remembers there were about twenty of them all crowding around, shouting and cheering him on and when John was finished hitting her, still with his back to the others, he shouted out with his head still down, to all of them to get back, as he was coming through. The class parted like a tide as he turned around and ran for his life out of the classroom and off out into the countryside. He kept on running across the fields to get as far away as he could.

Of course this was another excuse for dad to get out of school, to see if John was okay, because he knew most of his brothers hiding places. He would hide up regularly if someone had upset him. Dad was always looking for an excuse to leave lessons and get off out into the countryside. He asked the teacher if he could go after him to make sure he was okay. Mrs Green was still very upset and took it out on him, as it was his brother who had attacked her, but she eventually agreed to his leaving school, to find John.

Once he got home he found his mother didn't know of his brothers' whereabouts as he hadn't yet arrived and so he went in search of him in all the usual haunts. He was concerned about his brother and how he had finally really lost his temper in such an outburst.

There were some interesting places to hide in the countryside and dad thought he knew them all, but not this one until now. John was very good at hiding and his hideouts were becoming more difficult to find. It was a good thing then that he was so good at detecting them.

He eventually found him on the local farm in the cowsheds, beneath the tin lids along the rows of cow feeding bins. He was lying flat and very still so no one would ever see him beneath them.

When dad eventually found him he told him the school inspector wanted to talk to him. He recalls that John was in a mood for ages and as he continued to be stroppy, dad would only tease him more to get him out of his black mood.

In actual fact no teacher had ever reported what had happened and no inspector ever talked to him at the school or came out to see his parents. No enquiries were ever made whatsoever, although it happened probably at least three times more, but should not have done so.

Dad can never remember what Mrs Green had said to his brother which got him going. He thought she did it on purpose to wind up poor John just to see his reaction and he always acted as if on cue and ran off to hide up for a day or two. She would not have got away with it today and neither would have John. Dad said *"me and my brothers must have been right little heathens!"*

The boys got up to all sorts and each had their own talents, and one thing dad remembers well is his little brother's Hado and Willy's ability to run. He remembers they would all be sitting round the table eating their tea discussing what they were going to do when they had eaten and because dad had been given a bike by the school to encourage him to go more often, he would want to ride it around of an afternoon after school.

That bike had to be mended often as it got some very hard use. In fact it was replaced a few times over because of the harsh way he treated it.

He is not much better even to this day with his vehicles as they still get some rough treatment from him, often forgetting to top up the engine oils and ignoring the odd noises and warning lights on the dashboards.

Dad would then have been around eight years old and he would ask Hado or Willy if they wanted to go for a run with him after they had eaten. They were that keen to run, one of them always said *"okay"*.

Hado and Willy would run for as long as you liked alongside the bicycle and if anyone ever saw them about, dad would say to them that he was training them. He laughs at this memory as he told me he still doesn't know what he might have been training them for, as Hado was only six and Willy was only four. They had knots in cotton for muscles and would run like a whippet for miles, perhaps three or four without going red in the cheeks or even getting breathless.

Anyone who saw them would have laughed to see such skinny little boys bouncing along with such a spring in their step, quite happily for miles. Whatever they were eating it must have done them good, as they were as fit as fleas. When they got back they would easily have been able to go out again. They just loved to run. There was a long phase when they went out most evenings after tea and all enjoyed their time together.

Dad told me it took him a bit longer to enjoy running like that himself, but by the time he had reached his early teens, he was running regularly and entering competitions in galas and fetes that were advertised and held locally. These events were held regularly in the countryside along with many small festivals like those at harvest time. Remember this was a time before television or any high tech toys and children had to improvise with what they had. He enjoyed the regular runs of between three and five miles and would often win, sometimes winning a medal for his trouble. Occasionally he would run for a longer stretch but he was more comfortable with the shorter runs at this stage of his life.

He had his fathers' encouragement as he grew up and took to running a bit more seriously in his teens, which was when he was ranked as to his ability and then won more races in the area. Sometimes he got a shilling or two as his prize and he was very fit at the time and enjoyed it.

As the boys grew up their older sister Rene went to live with her grandparents. Perhaps it was thought that the influence of all those boys was not so good for her, being the only girl, but they all saw her regularly and she was still acknowledged as part of the family.

Being the eldest child of the family, Rene watched and waited for her little brothers to make their entrance into the world, and was often heard saying that she wanted *"a brown baby"*. In her innocence whilst out and about she had noted that there were in fact people with darker coloured skins and wanted one of those as a baby to play with as a young girl. She already had a baby doll but it was white and she wanted something different. The only problem being that the boys took up the word *"nigger doll"* and in their own innocent way translating it in their very broad Norfolk accent to *"Nida doll"*. It was unfortunate for her as her brothers were born mostly with fair hair and pale complexions, the last baby brother Edward (Nida) was born blond and blue eyed but the name stuck with him and she never got her wish.

All the boys would go out to explore the countryside around their home every day they didn't go to school. They would be gone for most of the day only coming back for tea because they were hungry after walking for miles around the countryside. If they wanted a drink there was always plenty of good clean water about in the rivers. They occupied themselves so well, getting engrossed in all that was about them. In the warmer weather they would go for a swim along the waterways thinking nothing of stripping off down to the bare flesh. In fact dad told me they all believed they were otters themselves as they considered the water as much their own environment as those creatures that lived there on the banks. They were surrounded by waterways, and had to cross them in order to get about. They were there so often, dad can't remember ever trying to learn to swim, having always played in the water, and wading in and out so often it was just another natural progression in the grand scheme of things. *"If you didn't sink, you swam"*.

He said as they grew older they would go and cut long thicker poles from the woodlands close by, so they could use them to vault over the eight to ten foot wide dykes when they wanted to cross without getting undressed or wet. Occasionally they got the pole stuck in the mud and got a soaking but generally it was a useful way of getting over the water. All the boys were very fit and natural athletes he tells me and it was just a game they played to get over the water and if they ever did get wet, none of them seemed to mind.

All along the main waters there would be small dinghy's left moored at various places and tied up. They would have been owned by the locals or holiday makers and not used too often by them. He thought the owners may sometimes have left them there to go off hiking or to the pub for a drink. The boys if they wanted to go out on the water would often *"borrow"* a boat to go out in but he did say they always returned it to where it had been moored afterwards. They would go out and do some fishing or meander about locally to see what was about today on the broads.

There were a lot of barges along by the waters edge and he remembers the gypsies painting pictures on the sides of them. These were the land workers of the day and in their own free time they would decorate the boats and barges where they stayed on the water. The painting was usually of the local wildlife, birds and flowers and he said they were all very talented artists and the boys would chatter away with them as they watched them work.

He remembers another time when he and his brothers found a swimsuit floating in the water. They had to fish it out with sticks and as they pulled and prodded it to haul it onto the sides of the bank, it stretched in size. It turned out to be a hand knitted bathing suit which probably had looked good on when it was dry, but as soon as the wearer had gone in for a dip would have expanded beyond all normal proportions. It must have been five foot long and at least three feet wide when they got it on the bank. Well, dad said they looked at it in wonder and then each one of them elected to try it on for size and eventually they all got into it together, at once, the crutch touching the floor despite its width.

He remembers a woman and a child came along by the waters edge out for a walk that afternoon and must have seen them trying on the bathing suit. It may have been hers and she could have been looking out for it and caught the boys trying it on. When they saw her they all jumped into the water to hide. They must have looked a picture when they were wearing it.

If the boys had no proper fishing gear they would tie a snare onto the end of a long sturdy stick and go along the banks very quietly, looking for a decent sized pike they thought could be had. They would sneak along the sides, often naked, ready for the dip that was coming in order to get it out of the water. They were ready to jump in if it was needed. They believed themselves to be otters anyway and when a pike was seen, the snare would be placed very carefully over the head or the tail and a sharp pulling action was made to try and catch it. Many a time the pike would turn out to be much too big for them to pull in and land. They were regularly about three feet long and it would often swim upstream with the pole and the snare still attached to it. Somehow the pike would escape from the snare. Later on they would find the poles floating, the snares sometimes still in one piece, along the waters edge, but no pike. Dad said he had to let them go as they were too big and strong for him or his little brothers, often the pike being longer in length than his youngest brother, but he recalls that it was fun trying.

OUT ON A LIMB

When not in the water the boys would make their own entertainment, which basically revolved around the use of a catapult and going out hunting for wild birds eggs from the nests, of which they had all made a huge collection. It was great fun looking for the nests in the first place and they got to know of most in the woodlands and hedgerows. It was always a challenge for them to find a new one but they were pretty expert at it.

He recalls on a number of occasions he would climb up the very tall trees to get rooks or crows eggs from the nests. The birds would always choose the tallest trees to nest in, sometimes quite far out on a limb. The tree would sway in the breeze as he climbed higher. He said he never felt at all worried about the heights he was climbing to or how the trees swayed from side to side, even how the branches bent and dipped, unbalancing the trees normal stature. Some of his school friends along with his brothers would watch him as he climbed up as confidently as a squirrel to the tops of the tall trees.

Some of the boys would like to try to attempt the climb themselves. Most however were put off their endeavour when he decided he alone would possess the only eggs from this source and duly peed down on the unsuspecting climber beneath him. He said on a number of occasions he even had to dive bomb them from the other orifice from a great height if the first attempt seemed to have failed.

It took a very brave kid to go up behind him and eventually it was declared safest to allow him the privilege of obtaining the crows eggs to barter with the others, getting his own way, using only natural resources it turned out.

He says he wouldn't attempt to climb so high today, but he can still climb a tree to some good heights if it was needed for the job.

He tells me he still looks out for different eggs in his territory, like a bullfinches nest in April in the blackthorn, or damson. Bullfinches make like a mini crows nests out of twigs and sticks and dad told me he will still keep his eyes open for anything a bit different and he's now in his seventies. Long tailed tits make lovely little nests and last spring he found six nests made of feathers and soft stuff like very dainty lichens, in his own garden. He doesn't blow the eggs anymore but it's still with him to know what's about, and to look for different nesting sites just as he's always done since he was a boy. He's just now more of an expert at it.

The young boys would have to blow out the contents of the egg by making small holes very carefully at either end. This was an art in itself and took time to do as their eager hands in the process could easily crush the tiny eggs. They would all take it in turns as they found a new egg, and when it had been completed successfully it would be packed in a small box filled with soft grasses and leaves to protect it. There were times when they tried to blow the eggs and there would be a part formed chick inside and the eggs would break open and smash. These eggs would have been sat on by the hen for a week or two sometimes. He says he didn't know any better then, as he was too young to know different.

They would take their spoils back home to be put into the old gramophone box they had sectioned out especially for the collection.

The boys would often swap an egg which they had gathered themselves to get a gull's or a guillemot's egg, because these birds didn't nest inland, only in their own territory, on the coast. They would often see the gulls flying over and coming inland to feed. The boys would always be after a different egg for the collection and some of their school friends had fathers that worked near the coast, and would bring them back eggs that they had found on the coast, so they could swap them, amongst themselves.

His grandfather on his mother's side of the family had a farm in the countryside near to Salhouse and his uncle worked as a gamekeeper on the same estate. His father loved to help out when he could and would let him tag along. When dad got accurate with his catapult and could pick off the rabbits quickly and cleanly at about eight yards away, the keepers wanted to take him along with them as well and would ask his father to bring him along when they went out to get the rabbits. His grandfather would always take along his lurcher dogs and if they saw a rabbit and the men with guns didn't get it, the dogs would give chase and get it anyway.

He recalls his grandfather carried a Norfolk paddle, and he said he hasn't seen one since that time.

It was a wooden tool which was anything from about four foot six, right up to six foot long, having a small hook on one end. The paddle end was used to dig out the holes in the sandy soil if they had sent a ferret down to flush out the rabbits; the ferrets would sometimes get stuck in the maze of passageways deep underground. This was when they needed to be dug out.

If a ferret had been attached to a piece of cord, before it had been sent down the hole and failed to come out again within a given time, the men would hook the line onto the paddle and give it a pull to get it out. In the line there would have been tied marker knots at regular intervals so they knew how deep the ferret had gone down.

The men would occasionally swipe a rabbit using the paddle if they were quick, to kill them as they came out of the holes.

Some times the terriers would get excited if they found a hole with a number of rabbits in it, often going in too deep and getting stuck in smaller warrens, unable to turn or back out in their excitement. They too had to be dug out. That's when the paddle would come in handy also. It was a useful tool for the keepers in that area as it was sandy soil and dad said he saw them use it a lot as a young boy.

There were so many rabbits about; the farmers would say they could only get half a ton of crops per acre.

They were a scourge of the land. There were so many of them and they loved to eat any fresh green tender shoots planted in the fields.

The farmers did not want or need the rabbits and because they were eating the young plants, they got the keepers to get rid of them by whatever means they could. The farmers would actively encourage anyone in those days to kill as many rabbits as they could because of this severe damage to the crops.

There was such a huge problem on this estate, the keepers used all the help they could get including snares and traps, nets and gasses and if this also meant using young boys with catapults then that was what was had. As dads' younger brothers all learnt to use the catapults they also went along as useful additions to the shooting parties. The keepers would also take along dogs and ferrets, as well as guns.

These days out getting the rabbits were dads' first introduction to shooting and he must have been very young, possibly three or four and he would have been expected to keep up with the men walking the estates and not to be a burden to his father.

It would seem dad was predestined to become a gamekeeper, because he said he never ever wanted to do anything else. He never really liked going to school very much although he was good at art and drawing and often had his pictures put up on the board to show the other kids how it should be done. He was particularly good at drawing the birds and wildlife that surrounded him every day of his life but he would always much rather be out in the countryside where he felt he belonged, amongst it all, and not in a classroom which made him feel like a caged animal. He loved the freedom of the open countryside, right from the start. It was his natural habitat.

ABSENT WITHOUT LEAVE

Dads' grandmother on his fathers' side was a gypsy. She was a tiny stunning looking woman as he recalls. She had long dark, curly hair, and always when he saw her she wore big, gold-hooped earrings. He remembers her quick flashing eyes, darting everywhere as she talked, having seen her only three or four times in his early boyhood.

It was always her who came to visit them and he thinks she travelled about, the family never knowing where she travelled to or from. She was a private lady only letting the family know limited facts about herself.

He rarely saw her, not knowing much about her or her family who travelled with her, and he was probably too young to have a real chat with her. He told me both his sister and one of his brothers took after her in their striking looks, although both are a lot taller.

Dad remembers his uncles, his dads' brothers, Edward and Walter.

Edward was a farmer locally and Walter was a cabinetmaker in Alfreston, Derbyshire, where the family originated from. He remembers he was a very smart man and was very much into wood and making all sorts out of it. He was heavily into the preservation of trees and of the countryside, having the same love of the land which follows throughout the family today.

His own father was called George White, but dad as

a boy got a little confused as to his real identity, since on occasions his father would call himself George Archer. This was because he had come out of the army without permission, having been a Grenadier Guard for a time, in London. He had originally signed up for six years and wanted to get out after four years. Dad recalls his father telling him he had worn one of those big furry hats, sitting on a horse at Buckingham Palace.

It would seem he found life too limiting and unexciting for him and could not stand the pressures of army life. He just left one day and never went back. Obviously he knew it was wrong but couldn't face going back and remained a bit elusive for years. Occasionally someone would come round and ask questions but the boys were told to say that no one lived there by that name.

It took dad a number of years to work out why he told people a different surname. Apparently his father never gave his real surname to the farmers where he worked in Norfolk and he never stayed to work with them very long. He moved all around the farms and estates as there was a lot of work about in general in those days. A lot of the young men who had previously worked there had been called up for war duties.

Dad recalls having a stamp collection as a youngster. He would collect stamps along with his brothers as the post came in. At school if anyone had something a bit different you could always be sure there would be a willing queue of kids who would barter for them as a swap. They also all collected cigarette cards of the day and would swap them with school mates to collect the entire sets.

His own father had hidden some of his paperwork

around the home; the paperwork contained his insurance stamps as well as some important documents which were personal to him only. He had hidden them away quite well he thought, underneath an old mattress in a room of the house where nobody else ever went, but boys being boys went in search of new adventures had found them.

This meant the boys had a collection of stamps that nobody else had and they swapped them at school with their friends for those they needed to make their collection even better. After all nobody else had anything like these. Their Mother eventually found out but it was too late by the time of the discovery. By this time the stamps were already stuck down into quite a number of local children's collections. They quite possibly are still around today in somebody's treasured stamp collection.

The boys didn't know any better he said and his mother just let the matter drop hoping it wasn't too important.

Every year or two a friend of his father's would come to stay for a visit and his father would always make an effort to look out for any work which might be around for him, making him very welcome into their home. This friend seemed to be a bit of a loner and lived rough most of the time. It turned out this man was a fellow escapee from the Grenadier Guards who took leave of absence at the same time as he, and both were afraid of being captured and taken back to face a probable prison sentence. His father being in a better position of living out in the countryside, miles from anywhere, with his wife and family, was less likely to be caught than his friend. His father would go round the estates at that time and do a lot of casual labour on the land, not having to give too many details as a lot of the work was paid daily, here today and gone tomorrow. There weren't so many farm hands during the war years and the farmers needed all the help they could get. He knew a lot of people too who would readily employ him and anyone he brought along with him when they needed some help.

His father was a very fit man and did some boxing. He was pretty good at it, being an all round sportsman and still played football well into his forties. He encouraged all his boys to take up sports such as running and boxing as they grew up. Dad remembers the huge gloves that he wore then, much bigger and bulkier than they are today. He thinks his father got his boxing gloves from the yanks at the airbase and they had most likely been swapped for rabbits.

FARM EDUCATION

During the war years it was illegal to rear game and to keep the hen pheasants for rearing. The keepers did get round this by salvaging *"dangerous nests"*, meaning those that were near the footpaths and on the roadsides. In fact it was anywhere they were likely to be discovered or walked near, and would cause the hen bird to fly away and abandon her nest if disturbed. These nests of eggs would be collected and taken home by the keepers, putting them under the broody hens they still had around. They would be safely reared and put back on the shoot when they were old enough and able to fend for themselves.

Dad told me he and his younger brothers went out to look for these nests in the breeding season and it just became second nature for him to pick up the eggs, taking them back if it was in a poor position. If it were a passable site, he would get some thick, leafy branches to screen them from view, away from the beady eyes of a scavenging crow or magpie. He would then keep an eye on the nest throughout the season until the eggs had hatched.

There were not as many magpies about at that time in the area because the keepers from the big shooting estates regularly dispatched them. Before the war had started these estates were heavily keepered, so having the resources to keep the numbers down. It was the same with the foxes and he can't remember seeing one when he was out and about in his earliest years. He was ten when he saw his first fox on the estate where he lived. It was also the year in which he got his first gun, remembering well his first shot at a bittern whilst out down near the waters edge.

Throughout all the younger years of dads' life he would go with his father, uncle and grandfather all around the local estates, when he wasn't at school, helping to do whatever jobs were needed at the time with the men. Some times it would be out in the fields on the sugar beet. He recalls his younger brothers also coming along as they grew older, to help out. His father must have been paid for it as the boys always worked well alongside their father. He remembers it was very wet sometimes on the fields and he was promised a pair of Wellington boots on many occasions but they never, ever materialised for him.

When he was out working with his father in the fields one of the older men who worked alongside him smoked and chewed old shag tobacco. He was called Fritz Box and he tried to show the young boys how to do the job. He could cut the tops off of the sugar beets without any trouble, a lot of the time not even seeming to look at what he was doing. He could probably *"do it with his eyes closed"* as he'd done this work for so many years, bending over without getting up from his stooped position for a long way across the rows in the fields. Going along the rows, every five yards or so to heap up the beets in a nice neat pile with all the points facing the same direction, he would also spit out the contents of his mouth regularly. Dad said *"I was sure he could knock out a fly at five yards with his spit"*. It must be a country thing as even he had a good aim.

In his break time he would light up one of his hand made cigarettes and on one occasion he asked dad if he wanted a smoke. Of course he was only young and all the men did it and so he accepted his offer of a rollup. The old man told him to take in a big breath as he drew in on the cigarette smoke and then to swallow it. Of course he did as he was told but lived to regret it immediately. He said his head spun and he felt sick in his stomach, reeling as it made him so dizzy. When he got home he still felt bad and couldn't eat his tea, vowing to never try a cigarette ever again. To this day he recalls the bad experience and said the old man did him a big favour as it certainly put him off smoking for life.

At the bottom of the stack yards along the sides of the lane close to their house there was a patch of plants the boys called French tobacco and they would roll it up to make a cigarette so as to blow smoke at the bats to make them squeak. He said he and his brothers would pull the tin roof up and slide it along whilst trying to unearth the bats from sleeping in the daytime. The bats would squeak as the boys filled their mouths with smoke and blew it at them. He said it was fun at the time although he knows better now. After the incident in the field with the roll up cigarette, he was never so keen to go and do this again to the bats, as he had learnt his lesson about smoking.

Dad recalls finding a dead turkey on the fields when he was out and about, and took it along to Spuddy Crane who would take anything they could find. He didn't know what the turkey had died of and said nothing, just took the money. Spuddy Crane would sell on what he got mainly to the Americans, even smaller birds like Starlings if they got them with their catapults.

A day or two after he had taken the turkey to him, Spuddy Crane paid a visit to his mother to show her what the boys had brought him along this last time. He said they all watched from round the edge of the corner of the barn, as Mr Crane stood outside of the back door explaining to his mother the boys had sold him something which wasn't quite right. He produced out of his pocket a huge ball of white meat twice the size of an orange. Apparently this huge lump had been found inside the turkey and would have most likely to have been the reason for its death. He was obviously angry he had given out good money for something that was not as good as it looked. He tried to get his money back from their mother but she couldn't help him, as it was the boys who had seen the opportunity and taken his money. Dad said they would most probably have spent it already anyway. Mr Crane went away unhappy that their mother hadn't given him his money back and dad says now he shouldn't have been so greedy and was well known for taking just about anything to sell on.

BEAST OF THE FIELDS

My father fondly remembers the time when he cut sticks from hazel to make himself a fishing rod, and one each for his little brothers. They had to go and dig for worms first for bait as it was their intention to go to the dykes fishing for the afternoon. They would always have their catapults with them anyway as they just might see something on the way which took their interest. They would often carry a spare hook or two and a bit of line for fishing as well. One of them also carried a small tin for the egg collection, just in case.

He remembers it was a warm spring day and they were on their way to the edges of the woods called the Pulk. There was a large sandy area which was a bomb hole and a kingfisher had made its nest in the sides of the crater. Each of them took a look and then in turn had a feel by putting their arm up to its full extent. Dad recalls his excitement as he felt six eggs nestled in the soft warmth at the end of the tunnel, deep inside the crater walls. He said the nest was mostly made up of very fine fish bones which felt soft to the touch; the kingfisher had taken small fish back to the nest to eat and regurgitated the bones, using them for the nests, then lining it with feathers. The boys decided they would take just one egg for their collection on this occasion. Having carefully extracted it from the nest, one of them carefully made a hole in each end and blew out the yolk, putting it into their tin to take home with them. As he was doing this, his brothers were taking aim at the rabbits which had congregated all about them as they had been so quiet at the nest, the rabbits having crept back to their sandy holes.

Next, they wondered slowly on to the riverside, dad and his brother John getting there first, putting their worms on the hooks. Very soon dad had a bite and quickly pulled out a perch.

A perch can be a tricky fish to hold as it has sharp spikes on its back and this one he told me was probably about two pounds in weight. It wasn't the easiest fish to keep hold of because of its spikey fins.

They had a dilemma as the fish was struggling a bit and they hadn't got anything on them to kill it with. He removed the hook and held the fish as best as he could, wondering what to do next. What with the fishes struggle and him trying to avoid being injured by the spikes, his brother John suddenly said *"I know how to kill it"* and promptly peed into its mouth whilst it was still being held.

Dad said he couldn't say if it worked or not because suddenly they became oblivious to anything else except for the sudden bellows and loud roaring noises getting very close. Coming towards them at speed was a very large and angry bull, only a hundred yards away when they looked up.

Farmers in those days put steel masks over the faces of the nastier bulls and this bull was wearing one. The mask was a form of safety measure by the farmers to deter and detract the bull from seeing too much of its surroundings.

It was also easily recognised by people walking about the farms that this was an animal which may harm you if you had to work near to it in the fields.

Just seeing this mask itself caused the boys to panic.

The bull was holding his head up at a slight angle so he could just see under his mask a little bit. If it hadn't been so serious it would have been funny.

"My God, I was scared!" he told me and the bull was getting closer and louder by the second.

Dad immediately threw the perch back into the water and flung himself off into the shallows of the river, as fast as he could. He thought it would have been him dying, not the perch if he wasn't quick enough. He landed in the bulrushes along the riverbank, trying to get away and hide in the undergrowth away from the bull, hoping it wouldn't see him in there, intending to swim across and out of danger.

By this time the bull had put its head down, pawing the ground, getting ready for a full charge, but he couldn't quite see exactly what he was charging at, luckily for the two boys at the time.

Dad had left John to his own defences in his panic to get away but looking back he could see he had run off and was now twenty yards away from the bulls' side, when he heard his brother John shout out to him *"I'll get him George!"*

You know that big dangly bit which hangs down between the bulls back legs, well, John had his catapult at full stretch by this time, taking very careful aim at it, letting the elastic go and hitting him smack on, right there.

The bull let out a huge bellow and continued its

roaring as it thundered off at full speed around the field and away from them, obviously in pain. They both breathed a huge sigh of relief that they were still alive, their hearts heaving, as they ran off to the safety of the woods, having completely forgotten about the perch and rods.

Dad said he had seen John pee on a few things before then, including a wayward Rhode Island red cockerel through some wire netting. He'd nearly lost his bits that day, but maybe he had thought the perch harmless, not realising this one had a big nasty bull as its protector.

GIVING A FLY A PARTING

As soon as the young keepers were called up to do their duty in the forces, most of the local estates were left with only a skeleton staff of workers. The rabbits reproduced so quickly that those who were left to work on the land had to help all they could with the culling. It was also a good cheap meat when there were rations and saved the day by being able to be sold, making a few pounds not only for the estate but helping the war effort too.

The Gin traps were used as another means of culling. These were legal in those days and were useful tools for the land workers and keepers. They would catch literally hundreds of rabbits every night and dad said he could hear them squealing as they were being caught in the traps as they sprang shut. He would go out with the men even at that early age and get the rabbits out of the traps. They would take out a paraffin lantern and visit the site hearing the traps go off so they knew where to go next. If any were found still alive they would be dispatched by a quick flick of the wrist to break the neck. He remembers hundreds of traps being set in the sandy burrows of the field edges and later on in the deep sandy pits, made by the dropped bombs of the German planes.

Only a few miles away from his home was an American Airbase, at Rackheath and as the war progressed the airmen infiltrated the pubs and were seen walking around the lanes near to their home. They were often seen riding a bike and would all pile out of the base at what must have been the end of their shifts.

This, it was found, by all the young boys of the area, was the place to be at the end of the airmen's shift, just outside by the gates. Dad said he would try to look nonchalant about it as though he was just casually passing, happening to be there at this time. As the men came filing out they would see the boys and ask them if they had any sisters. He would apparently pipe up,*"yes, six!"*

Well it became a bit of a thing if you said you had a sister, as they would give you some gum or even chocolate if you promised to bring her along to meet up with them the next night. He made arrangements many times for one of them to meet up with his sister which was never fulfilled.

He told me he sold his one sister at least six times a night whenever he went there. Of course, he never did as she wasn't like that and he never told her the full story. He told me they were so poor it was the only way he knew how to get some gum or chocolate in those days. You couldn't get anything like that in those days, as sugar was rationed but the airmen always seemed to have a plentiful supply of gum and chocolate and it was only natural to want to get some of it out of them. He had a sweet tooth and if it weren't going to the boys on the gates it would have been to someone else anyway, he told me.

His sister Rene did eventually end up seeing one of the airmen from the base called Steve but dad said it wasn't from anyone he tried to set her up with.

The boys would often go out for a wander around. They would all walk for miles looking for different birds, having a go on the catapults if anything took their fancy, stopping to try and hit a particular object to see who could get the closest. Occasionally they would have to go past the nearest church at Salhouse, which was about a mile away from home. There would always be a few birds, usually Sparrows to aim at on the edge of the church yard in the hedges and Yew trees there. The pathway home followed around the side of the church. They used this pathway regularly, which was cut into a natural dip along the lie of the landscape. The pathway went out for miles across the fields and was used by the locals to get to the church, from the surrounding farmlands.

One afternoon he and his brothers were coming back home from across the fields when they came across a young women walking towards them along the path. What a surprise she gave them because as they got closer they discovered she had bared her all, showing off her assets to the boys as they passed her by, her dress hitched up under her armpits and her black pants down around her ankles. He remembers her name even to this day but will protect her modesty by not mentioning it here. He said *"I had never seen anything like it before!"*

This happened on more than one occasion, dad saying she couldn't have been right, but did give the boys a real eyeful.

If the boys were feeling daring, when they neared the local church, they would sometimes go inside and take a look around. The first time that they ever went inside the church together, they were convinced they had heard strange noises and echoes that had no reasonable explanation as to what may have made them. He said on reflection it was probably the wind rumbling around in the high roof, and that fear had remained with them ever since. It really scared them to go inside having to dare each other in order to do so and they would run out in terror. Apparently they didn't venture that way too often, and would bypass the church if they could.

Looking for things to do after school, on the odd occasion, dad would meet up with some of the London evacuee's. He liked a bit of a challenge and the townie boys were full of themselves and reckoned they were fantastic shots with a catapult. It turned out that my father found himself taking on a bet with the mouthiest one. The bet was about who could get the most sparrows with a catapult, in a length of time, at the end of the school day.

This boy who was about the same age as dad and was pretty accurate for a townie, but not quite good enough. Dad got the edge on him and was declared the winner. He says now that this was only because he had the local knowledge of where he could go and get the most shots at the sparrows, because he knew where they would be. He might have bragged as a boy of eight or nine, but insists that anyone with the right knowledge could have done the same as he. He said the sparrows were collected up and taken home to be fed to the ferrets.

His own Father would sometimes take a couple of the boys along with him on the farms, when he went to work. They would help him out wherever they could and at his break times with the other farm workers, would make a bet for a woodbine cigarette. He would bet his boys could hit a fly on the barn doors using their catapults and a small pebble. Sometimes it was to hit a particular flower or even a blade of grass. One of the men would put a fork or spade out into the field and rest a potato on the inside of the "v" of the handle. Their father was so confident in their abilities, even little brother Hado at three and four years old was spot on and won many a cigarette for him from the unsuspecting work hands of the day. It was suggested by the men that each of the boys could hit their target with so much precision, *"they could give a fly a parting!"*

The boys would take independent bets on what they could hit, from the other farm workers in order to buy pellets for their airguns.

As they got older, dad remembers having a Diana airgun, and then a Cadet one, a Cadet Major and a B.S.A. The boys used all the guns as they grew into them but the only problem was they needed pellets to fire them. Picking off a target, after making a bet with the farm workers was more fun than working and they would win enough to keep themselves supplied with ammunition. The boys had grown up with the catapults and using air rifles was a natural progression as they grew older. All the boys were confident at hitting their targets no matter what they aimed at. They were born to hunt.

When their father took them out with the keepers they would take bets on being able to hit a particular sparrow in the tree. Dad said he knew he could always get a sparrow from eight yards if challenged like this and his dad would inevitably have his woodbines for the day.

COUNTRYSIDE CONNOISSEURS

The more practice at shooting they got, the better they became with their aim. And didn't they get plenty of practice. He told me he would take his gun out every day when he had the ammunition for it. If not they always had the catapults handy.

At this time he and his brothers decided they would shoot a variety of small birds to cook for themselves as they wanted to see if they tasted any good.

They would occasionally sneak a few matches off of their father when he wasn't looking and light up a camp fire out in the fields or woods.

The boys would go in search of a new bird to taste. Finding the new dish of the day flying about in the woods, the boys would shoot, pluck the bird and then skewer it with a sharp stick, turning it over and around in the flames until they considered it cooked. Of course it was sometimes very charred but he said they were always hungry and willing to try new meat.

On occasions they would try the fish they caught such as bream and perch or even a smaller pike, but he said the coarse fish had too many fine bones for them so they didn't cook them too often. They would often have walked for miles and be really hungry after all the exercise.

As they grew up, so did their knowledge, cottoning

on to what everyone else wanted to buy off them if they trapped or shot anything, having tried it themselves, finding it to be tasty and tender. They knew if they liked to eat it themselves then so would everyone else and they would always be able to sell it on.

None of them thought much of the blackbird and a moorhen tasted like town and country rubber tyres. When they considered they had tried quite a number of species of birds and fish they came across on their travels, they always knew they could go home and enjoy their mothers' rabbit stew every night, as it was always good and tasty. As they grew up they also knew if they got hungry they could always shoot a bird or catch a fish if needed, but only if Mother didn't feed them.

Sometimes when they were out and about the boys would find a wild bee's nest usually in the hollows of a tree. They would have spotted the bees hanging about the tree and those coming and going. If it was considered by the boys to be worth it, and time to take the honey they would go back home and find a sulphur candle that was hidden up at home in the sheds for such an occasion. The boys would light the candle putting it very carefully into the gap at the entrance where they had seen the bees pouring in and out, taking care not to upset the bees and avoid being stung. The burning candle gave off sulphur gasses that would kill all the bees in the stump or cavity of the tree. When it was safe and there were no bees flying about the boys would break open the entrance and remove sometimes huge quantities of combs, overflowing with beautiful wild honey, putting it all into the buckets they had brought back with them. The longer the beehive had been undisturbed the more honey it contained. He told me it was the best tasting honey in the world and they would sometimes take pieces of honeycomb to school the next day to chew on, making all their friends jealous of their find. It was something to be treasured at the time as it was quite rare to find a nest full of honey even then, but the boys did a lot of wandering around the countryside and knew where to look. He said there were a lot of wild bees in those days and it was far more common to find a hive then than it is today as there were more wild flowers growing naturally during his childhood.

Dad recalls he was partial to the brains of the rabbits when it was cooked but also added he wouldn't eat them today though. He said that no one gave him any opposition at the time when they sat round the tea table and he was left to eat what he wanted of those. It all tasted good to him as he said he was always hungry.

If dad had not got any rabbits for their tea the next day, he would sneak round quietly at dusk just before the keepers went out at eight o'clock and take some from the traps. He would set them again so they wouldn't know he had been there. He said this must have been his first time poaching but he did not see it like that as a boy because he thought of it as a necessity, in order to feed the family. He was quite under pressure even then.

BIRDS IN THE BEDROOM

The five brothers shared a huge bed every night. It was one of those big old brass bedsteads which had top and tail railing ends. When the boys woke up early in the morning even before it was light, they would go to the window and shout out *"Jack, Jack"* and then jump back into bed to wait.

The boys nearly always left the window open at bedtime in readiness unless it was very cool. Crows and jackdaws would sometimes come along to the windowsill of an evening as it began to get dark when the boys went to bed. It was a lot lighter for longer as it was double summertime. The birds were always hanging around waiting for the boys to feed them. They would never be far away, often just around by the house in the trees, and hearing the boys calling would come and sit on the windowsill, eventually hopping into the room, settling in a row, lining up on the rail ends of the big bed. Sometimes they would be there all night, for their mother to find in the morning. The birds would still be their hoping to be fed by the boys when they woke up in the morning and having become tame enough to sit there in anticipation of what may come.

Their mother would go mad when she found them, seeing the mess of the droppings on the floor all along the sides of the bed ends. She would try and get hold of as many newspapers as she could but at that time even these were a bit of a rarity.

The boys had fed the birds as babies by hand, taking over the feeding instead of the parents.

Originally they had taken these birds from their nests as youngsters. They talked to them as they were being fed, repeatedly saying *"Jack, Jack"* to them. They would open their beaks and the boys would drop tiny pieces of meat, usually ground up rabbit, and softened milky bread into them. When the boys talked to the birds as they were being fed, it was training them to know their voices, and teaching them to rely on being fed when called. It was because of this training, the birds responded to their calls as they grew up, flew off and learnt to be relatively independent in the wild. If the boys called out *"Jack"*, at any time when they were out and about outside, at least one of them would respond from the flock flying over. They would swoop down, often landing and sitting on their shoulders or sometimes their heads in the hope of being fed.

The boys would hang out of the window early in the morning if they hadn't seen the birds overnight, calling them onto the bedroom windowsill, much to their Mothers annoyance at the mess of it all, but it was a bit of a party trick at the time. Not one you see too often these days either.

Sharing a bed with his brothers had its drawbacks however in other more personal matters. He told me when the two youngest brothers wet the bed regularly he and John would tie a home made funnel to their bits and pieces along with a bit of tubing which hung down into the potty beneath the bed. Apparently this worked quite well on occasions unless they moved around a lot in the night. It did mean they all had a dry night occasionally. However my father informed me that after a while like this he would sabotage the events himself by tying a piece of string around the tubing to stop the water running down below the bed. He said it was sheer devilment on his part as he wanted to see the reactions of his brothers after all those dry nights. He would also make sure his brothers were well away from him and facing in the opposite direction on those nights so he did not have to suffer the consequences.

He and his brothers made plans as they awoke in the mornings on how to get out of going to school for the day as there was always something of far more interest to do out in the surrounding countryside.

It sounds a bit of a shame how he tells me he knew he was a good artist right from his first day at school. It was a natural talent. He says he was by far the best artist in his class when he was there and regularly had his work displayed up on the school walls for the other kids to admire. Amazingly he also admitted he loved to write, but felt there was such a lure to be out in the countryside he could not settle long enough to learn to be literate and to express how he felt on paper, although he eventually left school with average grades in English and always did well in any sport that was on offer.

The boys would start out as if on their way over the fields to school and on seeing the jackdaws and crows in the fields flying over would call out to them. Of course the birds would come down and sit on their shoulders in the hope of some food and the boys would walk home again to show their mother the poor birds were starving and so they could not go to school that day until after they had been fed. Often as not the birds would be still sat on their shoulders as they walked through the door at home. It turned out to be a regular great excuse for getting out of school.

The boys told their mother tales, saying it wouldn't be fair to leave the poor things all day without food, and the birds needed them and anyway they wouldn't be allowed to take them into their classrooms sitting on their shoulders like this. Their mother would have no choice with so much opposition. All those boys with such good excuses, and many a time they got their own way.

He recalls that on almost every Sunday in his early years, he and his brothers would go and see their grandmother and grandfather who lived locally on their farm. They had a pony and trap and would take the boys for a ride around the countryside near to their home. The pony was called Kitty, and he remembers she was creamy white in colour and she had a very gentle nature. He loved to ride on the cart, which he remembers was black, very shiny and quite small. They would have a chat with their grandmother as they gently trotted around the local tracks and roads near Salhouse. He recalls the pony passing wind a lot of the time on their journey, usually every other stride. Not so good when you had to sit behind it for too long. Apparently it happened every time they went out on a Sunday.

SPITFIRES AND HARVESTS

Each year in the summer dad remembers going out to the fields to help with the harvest as a boy. He had to help stack the sheaves of corn that were built up at the back of his home. Each one had a unique dolly on the top to show who it belonged to and each of the sheaves had a thatch put onto it to protect it and keep it dry. Of course there were always vermin that would make their home within such a huge grain store, and dad remembers watching the tiny, red harvest mice work their way round the edges of the stacks in the sunlight. They were fun to watch. There were also mice and rats that would live inside the stacks until it was time to break them open. This was when the wheat needed to be taken and thrashed out, ready for milling.

It was on these occasions that he and all of his brothers, along with the farm hands and helpers, would be ready and armed with a catapult, and a good supply of small round stones to hand, or an airgun. As the stack was broken open hundreds if not thousands of mice and rats would be milling around trying to find somewhere safe to run to, usually the next nearest stack. Everyone would just try to get as many of the vermin as they could to get the population down a little, and if all else failed they would resort to the use of sticks. Rats and mice would run up your trouser leg if they weren't tied up with string at the ankles so they all had to be prepared. The dogs were brought in as well as they would run after them and catch quite a few on their own.

Dad recalls one of the young men having a rat run up his trouser leg finding a space to get in through the waistband of his trousers. He shouted out to one of the others who quickly told him *"hang on I'll get my gun!"* In a panic the young man ran off after hearing this and was last seen halfway across the field trying to shake out his unwanted guest from around his nether regions.

The rats and mice were a big problem to the farmers in those years as they bred so quickly, having an ideal safe, dry place to live and plenty of food. Remember the sheaves still had the wheat in them and would still need to be thrashed out by hand after the rats and mice had finished with it.

At the back of the house were some farm buildings. Dad said he would be about twelve when he used to go out to the big old barn and climb up to the eaves. Using a stick, he would poke out the bats in the daytime along with any other animals and birds that he might find. He wanted to hear the squeaks as they came out. He did this out of sheer devilment and apologises for it now, regretting what he did. He did say though it was fun at the time.

Nothing seemed to be illegal in these years leading up to the war, and during wartime years everyone would have to fend for themselves as best they could. A lot of the time they didn't know any different. If it was illegal, there were so few other people around to put them right. They were miles from anywhere anyway and all the locals who lived there were farm workers and gamekeepers, instructed to do as the Squire or owners of the land told them. Game keepers were a law unto themselves in those days, as they were often instructed to get rid of the vermin that would disturb or damage the owners shooting on the land, doing whatever was necessary and no questions asked in those particular times. Poisons and traps and gasses were used regularly at the time and they could use whatever means they wanted to dispatch any bird or predator from the land and often they did. This has up until even the present day given gamekeepers a bad name in the community.

Things have changed a lot since the early fifties and there are many restrictions as to what can be shot or trapped, compared to the thirties and forties. The old Gin traps were made illegal and most poisons and gasses were banned from use. In those days there was an abundance of bird life in comparison and laws were put into place for their preservation, sometimes in opposition to the gamekeepers real thinking. There are a lot of natural predators out in the countryside who will pick off the small and young game chicks like the partridges and pheasants as they come out of the nests, and it was these that were and still are a big nuisance to the keepers who want to protect their young charges. These days nothing can be done to kill the bigger birds as law protects them, although there are fewer around.

Dad remembers Squire Wards was the owner of the estate that dad lived on as a boy and his parents rented the big farmhouse from him. He also recalls the neighbouring shoot was owned by a Major Trafford and was the biggest and best-known shoot in that area, employing a large number of gamekeepers on the estate before the war started. He would watch as the keepers brought back otters and occasionally badgers over their shoulders and dozens of rabbits on sledges, pulled by horses as they went past his house.

This all changed when most of the young keepers were called up for duties in the army and the forces from the local estates and dad had even more space in which to explore as there were so few staff to man the shoots. He would go out for the day with his older cousins and get all the rabbits they wanted and there was no one about on the estates to stop them. If they wanted a change they would go fishing or hunt around for nests in all the places that had been off limits.

Often as not he would have to leave his youngest brothers at home with his mum as they wouldn't be able to keep up with him as they would walk for miles and be out all day. Hado would have been only about two years old then and he recalls his mother shouting to young Hado to stay behind with her, *"come along Hado, you stay at home with me and play with your balls!"*

Life changed very little in the war years, but it did have its rare viewpoint on life in that things were done and seen then that the family had to adapt to and take in their stride. Living so close to the air base had its positives as well as the negatives.

Bombs were to be found all over the place, some unexploded, as well as incendiaries and butterfly bombs. Butterfly bombs had been thrown out of the German planes for the youngsters to investigate and pick up out of curiosity because they were interesting to look at. They would have blown your hands off if you picked them up, which occasionally was heard of. The boys would often find one or two on their travels about in the countryside and dad told me he once found a butterfly bomb in a tree, not far from their home. It was a cruel thing for the Germans to have done and all the children were warned not to touch them by their parents and the school. He said he considered aiming at the one in the tree with his airgun to see what happened but thought better of it and ran off home to tell his father.

It was ten years or more after the war with Germany when he went over there for himself in the army and seeing the damage which had been done to their countryside. The Germans had not rebuilt a lot of it even then. He said he will always remember seeing dozens of trains which had huge pieces missing, having ugly looking holes along their lengths from being bombed. They were all lined up in sidings. It looked as though it had only just happened because nothing had been done to dismantle them or to build back the bombed buildings over there in the smaller villages and towns. Even after all those years. He said he was quite shocked to see all this as it had been many years since the war and although they had dropped many bombs around and very close to his home in Salhouse it didn't seem nearly as bad as this. There must have been a few direct hits around at home but a few huge craters in the fields wasn't somehow too bad after seeing the extent of the damage to these towns all those years later.

There were a number of dog fights with the German planes over the house and dad recalls seeing the swastikas on the plane and the faces of the pilots looking at him through the cockpit windows as they swooped down low to avoid the Spitfires who were after them. Norwich was only a few miles away as the crow flies and these planes would have been heading across the coast to drop their bombs on the city.

He remembers he had gone out into the garden to watch what was happening because of the noise of the guns being fired in close proximity to their house. He said he saw no danger or felt no fear in standing there, watching this pretty horrific sight at so close a viewpoint. The small German planes were flying very low over the fields heading towards Norwich city and our Spitfires were after them as they flew underneath the barrage balloons that were dotted around, trying to avoid being seen and gunned down. Dad could easily have been mown down in the rifle fire but somehow he survived it all and continued to watch until they flew out of sight.

An incident he remembers well happened early one morning as they all lay in bed.

The boys were all lined up in bed still asleep as the sound of planes droned on overhead. He says it must have been just as it was getting light at about five o'clock. Usually it would have been the bombers from the air base coming back home, but this particular time was different. The noise was more intense than usual and got louder the more it continued, so much so that they had all been awakened.

They knew to listen out for the sounds which the planes made and wait for the engines to ease up, which meant it was about to drop its bombs. They lay there listening, sleepily, for the planes engines to slow, or carry on to another destination, never fearing they might ever be in any danger themselves.

Dad being the eldest was the heaviest of the boys and they all slept lined up in approximate ages in the bed.

Quite suddenly he watched as little Will being the smallest and lightest weight, flew up hitting the ceiling, still in his sleeping position, coinciding with the "whoomp" noise as a bomb hit the ground. Immediately he was followed in a cascade by the other four in quick succession, dad being the heaviest, leaving the bed last and not going so high, a fraction of a second behind each other. Each landed back down like a crescendo, or wave effect onto the bed. He said he watched it all happening in total disbelief and amazement. Thinking back on it all now he says it was quite funny as they all flew up into the air in a sequence. He knew that a bomb had been dropped very near to the house and this was the result as it made its impact with the Earth. This was serious stuff and the bombs were being dropped even closer to their home than ever.

It didn't do much for the glass in the windows either he told me as he remembered his father got him to help patch them up with card and wood temporarily later that morning. This was a regular occurrence in those days and he knew his mother and father must have been terrified every time the planes came over. They regularly lost at least half of the windows each time, but dad said he was too young to really feel as though he was in any real danger and it is only on reflection he realises they could all have been flattened along with the house at any time.

On this occasion he remembers they all got out of bed to see what had happened. They could not see much in the gloom of dawn, dressing quickly and going downstairs to have some breakfast of milky water and bread before going out to search for what had come down and caused the impact. They wondered if it was perhaps just a bomb exploding, although there had been a lot of other noises. They ran outside to find there were five bomb holes in the field right close to the house, all in a perfect row; obviously their house must have been a target that was missed by the German bombers this time. It was a lucky escape.

On another morning at the height of the bombing they were all awakened yet again by the sounds of the aircraft and guns going off. It must have been a particularly busy early morning, just before dawn, for the airmen on the base close by. There was a sudden commotion going on out there and the sound of lots of gun fire as well as the "whoomp" as yet another bomb had been dropped not too far away. They waited until the noises had stopped before getting out of bed. It was only just getting light and the boys all got dressed and went out after their hurried breakfast, running out and away to find what had taken place and made all the noise. They wanted to see if there was anything that had come down in the area.

They all ran towards billowing smoke across the fields, thick and black and still belching out, hanging heavy in the air. It was a German bomber that had been shot down which must have been hit by one of the local ground guns at the airbase.

The boys were first on the scene and found no signs of life in the plane or around it. The boys presumed that everyone was dead anyway. They seemed to accept the bodies and human spare parts they would see all around the remains of the planes, all of them taking very little notice of the gory scene that confronted them. They knew they could do little to help the German airmen as he told me they were always killed by the impact and were probably dead before they hit the ground anyway. The boys always seemed to get there before the police or services. After all the local police force was only one man on a bicycle.

Dad said the family were always on the look out for anything that might come in useful; they were like little scavengers looking to find whatever could be gleaned from the wreckage, and made use of at home. It seemed a bit macabre until he explained to me that his family were so poor, they could never afford any extras in life, and so, if they saw anything which could be useful, they would take it away. If it could be liberated, wasn't pinned down on these planes it was a gift. They would take whatever could be carried home and made use of by the family.

There were a number of items that were regularly taken from the wreckages of planes by the boys and in fact a number of the local school children also. They knew what planes to look out for because the tyres were better on particular planes, more so than some others. They would always go in search if they heard from any callers to the house that a plane had gone down in the area overnight. The boys would run across the fields along with the other local children to make their search of anything interesting. They went and got the tyres off the wreckage first if they could, as the rubber from the inner tubes was fantastically stretchy for catapults. The tyres would be broken open most times as it had hit the ground with such force, easily being pulled from the wreckage. They would grab a lump or two of the inner tubing to take home if they could pull it off.

The Perspex type plastic from the windscreens was often hot and it could be taken whilst still in its molten state and if you were quick, you could pull a bit off, or you had to snap it off if it had gone cool. This would have started off at about a quarter of an inch thick and small amounts were filed down and made into small models of spitfires and planes. Rings were made from these bits too by burning a hole in the middle with a hot poker from the fire and filing into shape. Some kids would even file patterns on it but dad says he wasn't as clever as that. A lot of the school children would sit quietly filing away and sanding their pieces of plastic in the playground, patiently forming them into different shapes. Some of them were very artistic with it. Dad told me he had a go at this but he wasn't as good at it as some of the others.

Dad recalls his father coming home from work not long after this, with a finger he had found whilst on his way home from work. He had found some paper and had wrapped it up in this. The boys presumed, as did his father that it had come from one of the poor airmen who had crashed. Dad said he couldn't think why he brought it home with him that day or even what for, and thought he would have disposed of it himself.

During the dogfights over the village of Salhouse, one of the horses was fired upon in the fields, but lived to tell the tale by still working on the farms pulling a cart. Dad recalls seeing a row of six bullet holes all along the sides of its body in perfect precision. It had been hit by one of the planes who had also fired upon the village school. In those days a horse was considered to be of great value as a worker and had obviously undergone some trauma but it was not its time to go then and dad said the man who kept it was a forester. The horse was in no way distressed and he wondered if the bullets were still inside its body. He also said that if this had happened today the horse would have been put to sleep.

EXERCISING CATS AND DOGS

Dad described another activity that he and his brothers would sometimes get up to after school.

He told me they had always got dogs and ferrets to go out with if they wanted to. Their Father kept twenty five to thirty ferrets in the sheds he had built by the house. The ferrets were used regularly by the men to send down the holes to flush out the rabbits which were netted or shot. These ferrets were used by all of the boys when they went out as well as by their father. The ferrets also had to be fed as well as the family and the boys had to go out and get meat for them every day. They would feed them on birds like sparrows, pigeons and starlings or whatever was the target of the day by the boys. You couldn't let up, as there were so many of them to be fed. If a ferret gets too hungry, they would not be good to take out as they would often look out for their own dinner first, but if you kept them fed a little every day they would always be keen to get more and flush the rabbits out efficiently. His father would tell the boys to shoot a ferret if it did not flush the rabbits properly, since the ferret had to prove its worth as did all the other working animals. The family always kept a few dogs around the place too as they were used as tools in the countryside during these times. They were normally Norfolk Lurchers and were very popular in that part of the countryside for running the rabbits.

Apparently most of the keepers and those that worked on the land kept these dogs as they were ideal for the job. They had a number of dogs at home throughout his childhood and he didn't get too attached to them as they were working dogs and lived outside in the sheds and kennels at home. He soon realised as he grew up which ones were best for him, some more than others would respond to his calls as they worked with him. He reminds me they always had to run something in order to catch something, because it's what his grandfather had taught them all from an early age.

They would get out of school, that's if they had gone in the first place, and when they got home, finding there were no rabbits in the field close to the house they would do something a bit different. They invented their own game, he says, reminding me that in those days nothing was illegal. He went on to recount his early afternoon games with the rest of their pets.

The family had two pet cats called Mona and Freda. The boys would go and find these and make such a fuss of them and be real nice to them. They would scoop them up gently, one under each arm and take them to the centre of the field by the house, about two hundred yards out. He said the cats knew what was going to happen to them next, sometimes struggling in their arms where they had to be held tightly, as they had done this quite a number of times before.

Of course the boys had grown up surrounded with dogs and the two cats at home. They were used to taking the dogs hunting with them whenever they could.

One of the boys would have taken the lurchers, on their leads out to the field and held onto them. Then it was time to let go of the cats as they ran off knowing what was coming next. The boys would let the dogs go the second they were down and they of course chased the cats. Never mind hare coursing, the boys had their own way of keeping the dogs fit, cat coursing.

The dogs never caught the cats, they knew them, but would give them a run for their lives all the same, and he said they never found the cats in the same place twice after that. They were never injured whilst this took place, but boy could they run. The dogs had a good run too and were fit and keen to run after them; it was just another thing for them to chase.

As it was getting dark, dad and his brothers would go looking for the cats to make sure they were okay and to make a fuss of them, hopefully having forgiven him and his brothers after their terrifying ordeal. Sometimes the cats hid in the farm buildings away from the house but would come home to be fed if left to their own devices. They would have been far more afraid to go home if the boys hadn't made such a fuss of them afterwards, but he recalls they were always wary of them, even when they were taken up to the bedroom as the boys went up to bed.

Just to make the cats life even more difficult, if their mother heard they still had them in the bedroom later at night, still fussing over them, she would shout out to them *"put those bloody cats out!"* and one of them would pick up the cats and open the window, and just chuck it out. Luckily cats always land on their feet. Never mind having nine lives, they needed a hundred at least. Dad said they all loved them both even though the boys gave them a hard time. Those poor cats, at least they got plenty of exercise.

They were all too busy trying to avoid bombs dropping in those days and he was lucky enough to still be alive himself today to tell these stories and have a laugh and smile at the memories. He reminded me everything had its place and its use in the countryside in those days, whether it is bird or animal and he reminded me, neither were there the restrictions that there are today.

The family also kept a few pigs at home. He told me they were the skinniest pigs he'd ever seen and looked like greyhounds. You could see their ribs. He told me he always collected the acorns in the autumn when they dropped, for the pigs to eat. All the boys would go off together into the surrounding woodlands, sometimes collecting their tin bath full to the brim. They went out daily at this time of year until they had collected them all in the area.

He reckons his father must have sold on the acorns without the boys' knowledge which is why their pigs were so skinny.

It was years later he first saw a really well fed pig and realised that pigs are in fact meant to be big and well rounded in appearance. He told me he was quite shocked when he saw later on his life how big they could get if fed well.

THE BOYS MENAGERIE

One of dads' cousins was called Rusty. He was one of five boys born to his mother's sister, and they lived fairly close to them at Salhouse. Rusty had a bond with my father, always seeming to have more time for him than the others.

Rusty was older than dad, both having such empathy with the countryside and the wildlife. He seemed to have patience with him and took the time to show him things the other cousins never had time to.

His cousins' ages ranged from thirteen to twenty, and dad and his brothers were three to ten, dad being the eldest.

Rusty was very good with the catapult as well as the mouth organ he played around with whenever he could, messing about. Dad said *"he could make it talk."* All his cousins he recalls could play the accordion as well, which he particularly liked even at that young age. He tried it himself along with the mouth organ but felt he wasn't as talented at it as they.

Dad was a good listener and learned all sorts of things from Rusty. He went with him more as he grew up, joining in more with his cousins' antics and learning even more about the ways of the countryside.

These boys had also grown up amongst the same conditions and went out with the keepers long before dad was born. They had got to know the ropes and if you wanted to know anything all you had to do was ask one of them; they had been there and done it all. All of them could shoot well too.

They would regularly go out rabbiting along with the keepers and started to take dad along with them, as he was so accurate with the catapult.

These boys would go along to the stack yards and shoot the sparrows that were around. There were thousands of them in those days and they could shoot them all day long and there seemed to be no fewer about for it. The sparrows were a nuisance, as they would eat so much of the seed the farmers planted in the fields. In those days the seed would be left nearer to the surface of the soil as it was scattered by hand. It wouldn't have been covered over as well as it is today.

The boys could happily use these sparrows as target practice with full permission from the farmers. Those that they did not shoot, they hopefully scared away. Younger brother Hado, he says would hold his gun in a particular way which looked a bit awkward as it was too big for him but somehow it didn't affect his accuracy in any way. He held it almost at his waist bending over to see down the barrel as best he could. He eventually grew into the gun.

When it was time to cut the corn in the fields in the summer, dad and his cousins would all make their way over to pick off the rabbits as they came out of the upright wheat as it was being cut.

When the farmers cut the corn they would do it from the outside edges of the field. They would go round with the horse drawn binder, with flails, setting the shocks upright into eight sheaves at a time. As they were going round the field, those with guns would shoot the rabbits that bolted out of the corn towards the hedgerows. Dad said he would prepare whilst he was waiting by getting a bucket of small, good stones and then aim at the rabbits with his catapult, as they appeared at the edges of the corn. A lot of the rabbits would wait in the upright corn as the horse and men went round and round, the area getting smaller.

Of course you had to be careful about where you aimed and couldn't fire a gun anywhere in the direction of the farm workers. This meant all the boys had a free for all as the rabbits first appeared and only those with guns would fire on those that made a run for it. The rabbits would come to the edges of the corn and sit very still, getting ready to bolt across to the undergrowth of the surrounding hedgerows to make their escape. He would walk quietly round the edges of the upright corn and pick them off as they popped up. He had time to aim and fire straight at the head, the rabbit flying up into the air and falling down flat as he hit them regularly *"in the nut"* as he put it.

Using only a stone to kill a rabbit in the head meant the skins were good and clean, having no bullet holes in them. The boys could sell them for their skins if they wanted. As they all got older it became a new way of making a bit of extra pocket money for them.

The farmers would get sixpence each for these rabbits as normally it was only four or five pennies for each one. Dad said he would try to keep a few back for himself some days so he could sell them on for himself. He would even have a go at getting starlings at twopence a time if he could.

Around this time, despite the turkey incident, dad

had made friends again with Spuddy Crane who was from Wroxham and would still buy just about anything dad could shoot with a catapult, because it was nearly always a clean kill. At this time it was difficult to get meat because of the rationing, except the rabbits, and this man took whatever he could get off him. He would even give twopence for a blackbird and if he got a milky doe rabbit by accident would have these too. No one else wanted them.

Dad said when he was about ten he took two lurcher dogs from home with him, going off to get some rabbits for himself. He recalls on this occasion having already got thirty-four in the afternoon with some of the other boys, he wanted to carry on after they had all called it a day and gone home for tea. He was still feeling keen and set off on his own, along with two of the dogs. Because it was double summertime it was daylight until very late in the evening so he felt he could make use of the daylight hours as did the farm workers getting in the harvest.

On his return home late that night his father told him off for wearing out the dogs that were shattered after all their running.

Dad had said the dogs had got so tired out that they were walking over to the rabbits to pick them up and sitting down to take a rest as the evening progressed. They could hardly move one foot in front of the other with tiredness when he eventually brought them home, as they must have run for miles and had worked the whole day without a break. Having had such a scolding from his father for overworking the dogs, dad learnt a very valuable lesson in the care of working dogs. He remembers though they had helped him in getting ninety-four rabbits in that one evening, a figure that at least he was very proud of.

The Father of his cousins was called Chink and he was permanently drunk and as dad put it *"you could smell him half a mile before you saw him and then another mile after he had passed you by!"* Just occasionally he would be on a bike, that's if he could ride it, keeping his balance.

Dad never knew his real name but he worked on the local Horning ferryboat. He remembers he always wore a brown Harris Windsor tweed check suit, and a dark brown Windsor hat. He had an old boat and for sixpence a time he would haul you over the water by a chain at Salhouse. Some people would try to haggle with him over the price, but he wouldn't give in too often. While he waited for customers he would go to the local public house right by the waters edge. He couldn't have been too busy because he seemed to spend a lot of time in there.

It was quite a few years later that a picture was printed of him doing his job as ferryman on the front cover of a country magazine, The Field, and my father recognised him at once as he was dressed the same as he had always been.

When he was finished for the day or too drunk to do his job, dad would sometimes borrow his boat with one of his brothers or cousins. Even if it were daylight they would go armed with lengths of chicken guts and a huge ball of wool to go babbing for eels. They would thread the chicken guts onto great long lengths of wool, then tie it to six foot poles and drop them over the sides of the boat, until it hit the bottom. The eels would attach themselves by their teeth three or four at a time. He said he could feel them pulling and moving about. He would haul them in and throw them into the bottom of the boat until it was writhing in eels. Some of them were apparently as thick as his wrist. He doesn't recall what they did with the eels they caught but someone will have bought them off the boys as he says there were so many of them to deal with.

Quite regularly his brothers or cousins and himself would walk down to the broads and see if they could catch a pike. To do this they first had to catch some smaller fish to be used as bait.

This was the easy bit of it all as the pike, when he had caught them were often nearly as big as he, weighing probably around twenty pounds each, maybe more. These were monster fish to land for a young boy of eight or nine, with their rows of evil looking backward facing teeth. Some pike were as big in size as his brothers.

Often as not dad said he was so scared at the way the pike looked at him that he wouldn't reach inside and get the hook out of its mouth. It was by no means an easy job to land this huge creature after their long tug of war, and when he did hook one, it was another thing to have to reach inside of its mouth with his hand at any stage. All those dangerous looking teeth so close to his fingers, and then only to get a hook out. If he could he would get a stick and push the hook back through but this wasn't always successful. Sometimes the pike would swallow the hook.

Sometimes he was that scared of the biggest ones he would abandon the whole lot, rod as well and run off home, to find something a bit safer to do.

He told me he would often go round his cousins' home to see what the older ones were getting up to that day.

He said he remembers walking into their kitchen to see his cousins. He would stand to listen and look on in awe as a row of tiny baby goldfinches, were all lined up around the kitchen sink, along the pipes and on the window ledge, singing beautifully like little tinkling bells.

They were such perfect, tiny birds with golden yellow stripes, with red round their minute beaks. It was a site to wonder at, and he said he would just stand there for ages looking and listening to the very pretty sound they made. The young goldfinches sat there, in a row, relaxed, unfazed, and obliviously happily singing, although they could have flown off if they wanted to. It didn't seem to matter who walked into the room, they continued with their heavenly song. This is one of his very happy memories of that time and he says he has never seen anything quite like it since those years.

His cousins had tamed the young chicks after they had taken them from their nests at a very early age, just a little while before they were ready to fly. They would take the babies and put them in cages allowing the mother to come along and still feed them, through the sides of the cage. The babies would all get used to seeing the boys and being in close human contact. When the boys were able to take over from the feeding they would do so with seeds. The birds got used to being handled, but sparingly and the young goldfinches would entertain them with their birdsongs around the house and in their own kitchen. The boys would allow them their freedom once they reached maturity. Everyone loved to have these birds around the home and looked forward to hearing birds like these every spring and early summer.

His cousins were well known locally for taming wild birds and whenever dad went over there he would find new birds hatched out by them, depending on the season, some of them bigger like ducklings and partridges which they had in various pens about the property. They found nests out in the fields, bringing home the eggs if they thought they needed to be cared for. Sometimes the nests had been abandoned. They would put these eggs under a broody hen until they hatched. His cousins always looked after them well and released them back to the wild when they were fully grown. They were just naturals when it came to looking after young chicks and any game eggs they found in their wanderings around the countryside. The cousins passed on their expertise every time he visited them.

Dad it seems had similar tendencies with the crows and jackdaws, having learnt from his cousins the art of taming wild birds. It must have been in the blood. He mentions again that he was never bored in his young life and can never remember not having something that needed doing. Even in his youth he says there was never enough time in the day to do what he really wanted. It was also a great time of discovery and recalls it was on one of the waterways he said he stood over the edge and watched as a water hen dived down into the water to look for a small fish. A water hen will not surface, if it sees it may be in danger from a predator, until the coast is clear, which is usually not too long.

He stood and counted the minutes as the bird did not resurface. It must have seen him standing there watching and waiting as its breath ran out and it floated to the surface.

He says this only happened the once as he realised what had happened. He had learnt from the experience.

THE LODGER EXPERIENCE

Times were pretty tough financially, he tells me, with is parents. Whatever his father earned on the local farms and shoots, had to be enough to go round, putting the food on the table and paying the rent, not to mention all those boys' trousers and shirts.

His parents found it necessary to take in what he calls a brace of lodgers.

Peggy and George Shepherd came to stay in the big farmhouse with them to escape the bombs in London for a short while. Apparently it was still considered safer than being in London. They were a pleasant couple who fitted into their home without too many problems. Taking in lodgers was a way that his parents could make a little extra money as the boys were growing up and they certainly had the space in their home for it. They had a number of rooms they never used for themselves because the farmhouse was so big. It was considered a bit easier way to make money than the boys having to have to go and get some rabbits to sell for cash. His mother could not afford the few shillings every couple of weeks for one pair of boys' trousers they seemed to get through so quickly.

The couple paid his mother fifteen shillings a week board and lodging, and it was very welcome. They stayed happily for a few months.

Dad said Peggy was not the smallest of women, a kind of sturdy, chunky build. The boys including him were always looking out to have a bit of a laugh and giggle and they found when she went down to the ladies long drop at the end of the garden they could spy on her through the chinks in the wooden slats and tin of the building. There was a long drop toilet for the men and one for the women. One was made especially for all the kids as well, but much smaller.

The boys would sneak out after seeing her get up and on the move towards the door to the garden. They would sneak round the back along with lots of sniggers and giggles, looking on the way for a long piece of grass or thin twig or corn to poke through at her. Sometimes they got hold of a long feather.

As she sat on the seat they would be trying to poke her in the rear, suppressing their laughter and giggles as best they could. If she ever knew they were there, she never said as she was a good soul, but all the boys had some fun with her in the time she stayed.

Another guest they had a bit later on was quite in contrast to Peggy and George. He was a lot older, well into his seventies although dad said he could have easily have been a hundred and seventy. He always wore a huge black coat which had a cloak attached to it and a black wide brimmed hat. He also always smoked a clay pipe. He looked as though he was someone from another age at least a hundred years before his time, just in the way he dressed. He was very quiet, never speaking very much and all of the kids were scared of him, probably because he looked so dark, dressed in black and looking so serious all the time.

There were a few spare rooms in the house, it was so big, and all along the length of the house was a tunnel that led to the dark lodgers' room away from the family. Along the tunnel on the corner, was a huge old brass fronted oven which had to be lit daily. The boys would try to avoid this area and if they saw him whilst fetching the firewood for the oven, and would run like hell. If he were seen around the house generally, they would always run to get away from him. He said *"he looked so terrifying!"*

On one occasion, dad was out with his brothers who had been sent to the shop for a loaf of bread for their fathers' lunch for the next day. They were on their way home, chatting away, and picking out the centre of the loaf as they walked home. Dad said they were always hungry. They would often have had only a piece of bread about the size of his thumb on reaching home for their father, but he insists that being hungry, it was too much of a temptation to carry a still warm loaf home all that way without having a bite or two each. He said his mother never got angry with them although as soon as they handed the remains to her they always bolted as fast as they could, just in case.

On this one particular day, they spied the new lodger in the distance, walking towards them along the road.

The boys were scared as soon as they spotted him and didn't want to have to walk past him. They discussed alternatives to avoid him but came up with none. Then matters took their own course of events.

As he walked towards them he could be heard muttering to himself, which sounded a bit weird. He said *"oh no, not again, you always get me like this."*

When he was within feet of them, he suddenly tottered

backwards, arms in the air, falling flat on his back, cape and coat splayed all around him. His hat landed right beside him along with the big square woven straw bag that he always carried. Normally it would have been over his shoulder but not on this day. He just lay there flat on his back, motionless.

The boys just stood there amazed at what had taken place, rooted to the spot in fear and astonishment. Breathing again, suddenly they found their feet and flew off towards home with the nearly eaten loaf of bread as fast as their legs would carry them, never once looking back to see what happened to him.

Dad said he can't ever recall seeing the old man again around the house after that episode and on reflection he believes he may well have had some sort of seizure or fit. For all he knows he could still be laying out there, to this day. In those days there was so little traffic on the roads, he would have had very little chance of discovery.

Life went on, as normally as it could despite the war which continued, but times were hard and there was very little money to spare to buy clothes and shoes for five boys. It cost his mother four shillings and sixpence for each pair of new trousers every time the boys wore the knees out, and that was quite regular. She only got about thirty shillings a week income to keep them all fed and clothed.

When he would go along with his father to the farms to work, he would take along his airgun and walk along by the side of the Shire horses ploughing. He told me he would shoot a peewit or two, who flew in to get the worms from the newly turned over soil, as he and his father quietly walked around the fields.

He remembers a peewit tasted pretty good even when he and his brothers had tried cooking them over a fire when they went out nesting, albeit a bit on the small side, and he could always sell them on to the American airmen from the nearby base, as they said they tasted just like partridge, and were about the same size too. They would give him a couple of shillings for each of them. He said he would also occasionally shoot a blackbird or a water hen whilst with his father in the fields, as turning over the soil attracted all sorts of birds as they walked around. If he got a few birds over a couple of days, he would walk the four or five miles to Spuddy Crane in Wroxham who would always buy them off him for a few pennies each. It was all extra pocket money.

On his arrival home one afternoon from a hunt about, he found his little brothers Hado and Willy upset. He had stumbled upon a gory scene close to the woodpile at the back of the house. Apparently little Willy had been trying to help his older brother Hado chop some kindling for their mother. They had been out to the shops to buy some groceries and on arriving home, mother had asked Hado to cut a few sticks to light the fires in the house. Hado was only four and Willy nearly two. Hado had previously found this no problem. He was good with his aim and had often watched his older brothers chopping the sticks for kindling, when previously the boys had allowed him to have a go at it himself. Little Willy had also wanted to help and stood and watched for a while. On one of the downwards strokes he had made a grab for the piece of wood to hold it steady for his brother. Along with a splinter of wood, Hado accidentally chopped off three of his little brothers fingers. They were hanging by threads of skin still and on hearing the screams and shouts of the two boys their mother had rushed out bringing a towel with her. She immediately wrapped the towel around the hand, scooping up all the fingers along with it. Hado ran off very upset at what he had done. Dad went and found him and took him off whilst his mother dealt with the injuries.

Dad then took Hado off into the woods to try to distract him from the situation. He told him they could go and try to get a few pheasants and check on a few his snares. Both of them still recall watching from the woods as an ambulance arrived to the house taking away their little brother and mother to the hospital. Neither of them can now recall how their mother got the help of the emergency services at the time as they lived so far out of town then. He presumed there must have been someone around who got on their bike to make the call up in Salhouse.

All turned out well for little Willy. Within a few weeks his fingers had healed and dad says to this day he can never remember it having a lasting affect on him. The doctors must have successfully sewn back the fingers as parts of them were still attached by skin and blood supply. Luckily they all worked. Dad said it would have been because his mother had gathered the hand in the towel within seconds of the accident, which was a blessing.

Hado told me his big brother always looked out for him as they grew up and would do anything for him as a child. All the little brothers were always looked after by him and no one was excluded unless they were too young to be able to go off on long walks to get some rabbits and game birds.

When dad got a pheasant even if it was an older cock bird he would take it to the Americans first as they would give him enough cash to go and buy some more pellets and would occasionally give him up to four cartridges as well.

The airmen would shoot clay pigeons on the edges of the base. The gunners would practice shooting moving targets and they were pretty good at the skeet clays. As a consequence it meant that the gunners would always be able to lay their hands on a few cartridges for whoever got them some delicacy they fancied.

LITTLE SCAVENGERS

On the air base was also a huge dump from the American airmen. There were all sorts to be discovered, including clothes and shoes. It helped their mother out by getting a few new second-hand clothes. There were some less suitable items than others, but you had to have what fitted best. The Americans threw away some good stuff which could still be made use of. They could often bring home a pair of good G.I boots and shoes, even if they were a bit too big for him and his brothers, at least they would fit someone in the family. The boys had to keep their eyes open for whatever they could make use of at home. Rummaging around they often had a problem with only being able to find the one of a pair of shoes or boots.

Dad said he went to the airbase dump when his father took the dogs on the edge of the airfield looking for rabbits. His Father would go round the huge piles of bombs on the side of the tip and net the holes along the sides where the rabbits lived. Dad would have a good rummage around whilst his father hunted.

He remembers finding a wonderful black pinstripe suit. He tried it on right there and found that it fitted him perfectly. He decided he had to find a pair of smart boots or shoes to complete the outfit. He couldn't find anything suitable on that occasion but remembered he had a pair of long black knee high leather boots at home he had got on his last visit. He thought they would go well with the suit and would make a great outfit.

When he got home he tried on all his gear together and decided he looked pretty good. He had tucked his pinstriped trousers into his knee high boots, the heels of which produced a wonderful clicking sound as he walked. He stomped around and he said he thought he was *"the bees' knees"* in his getup, feeling very proud of his new outfit.

He felt so good about his new outfit that he wore it to school. He said he felt marvellous, as everyone would look at him. He believed himself that he looked impressive in it. What reinforced this were the stares that he got from the other kids and anyone else who saw him dressed in this fashion. He seemed to get a lot of attention over his new look. He told me *"I must have looked a right prat!"* as he stomped about like a German Gestapo, clicking his heels on the wooden school room floor. His teachers never said anything to him about his new clothes but he wonders what they really thought about his look.

Quite a number of the other school children wore clothes they had liberated from the air base dump and it became a common occurrence as the war progressed.

He wore the outfit for about a month, which was until his toes started to poke out from the front of his boots and they became too uncomfortable to wear. The suit on its own didn't look so impressive without the boots and after that and he went to find another from the same site. *"Easy come easy go"*.

On another visit he remembers going to the same army base tip with some of his brothers, without his father. They would have a good root around and on this one particular day they found an intact Vary light. They had discovered them on previous occasions and taken whatever bits of it that were lying around. Sometimes they would only take the stick-like candle if it was found on its own at the dump, having already become detached from the large main body.

Vary lights were used by the pilots as a distress signal if they were in trouble during a flight and were set off using a gun that went with it. It would give off a huge red light which when activated would light up the sky like a beacon, and you would be able to see it for miles around. It was in fact a flare which would continue to burn quite fiercely for some time.

On this occasion they had found the vary light and dragged and carried it over to the woods to see if they could scrape off some of the candle bit which stuck out from the main body of it. They had removed the candle piece on other occasions previously, having found if you scraped a bit off, and put a match to it, it would light up and burn with a bright light, giving out a hell of a flame on its own. This part was thought to contain sulphur.

They would try to pull the whole thing off if they could. It was often still very well attached and on other early evenings had entertained the boys for a while, quite nicely trying to take it apart, and done no real harm.

This night however was a different matter.

What they had failed to do was to remove the candle structure completely before lighting it, so taking it off from its body that contained the main red flare.

They were too near the edges of the woodland when they lit the flame and it burned so fiercely that they all got scared of its intensity and ran away back out into the middle of the field. It was too late to move it once it had started to burn.

It was out of their control now.

Realising they could do nothing but watch, they had all run like hares having thrown themselves face down in the field, laying as flat as they could, waiting for the inevitable.

When they looked up on hearing the noise they knew it had detonated, sending out a bursting shower of flames towards all the nearest trees setting them alight at once. The Vary light glowed brightly, lighting up the entire sky and burning the trees so intensely that the boys were terrified and didn't know what to do. The whole side of the wood quickly caught fire spreading along its length in only a few minutes. They just lay there, faces down and wet themselves in terror. They were sure to be found out, as it would have been seen for miles around. It looked to them as though the whole world was on fire.

The boys stayed there for a while to see what happened and witnessed the destruction of most of the woodland, knowing it was on their grandfathers land, also knowing this was so big they would never be able to admit to anyone what they had done, even though it was an accident.

After a while they got up and ran home, all looking the worse for wear and certainly feeling it. Even they knew they smelt no better than their grandfather's Billy goats that were tied to the bottom of his garden. This was not only from their pants but also from the fumes of the sulphur, being so close to it as the vary light exploded.

Not one person said anything to the boys although

they may have suspected them, quite probably their mother who had to wash their clothes, which on evidence alone would have put them very close to the spot in question, because of the sulphur fumes. Dad was too scared to admit what they had done at the time and is only now today coming clean about it. There were lots of questions from their parents at the time, but they had stuck together through fear, in the hope that this sorry situation may have eventually been blamed on the Germans.

There were a large number of barrage balloons in the skies around their home, being so close to Norwich as the crow flies and searchlights were regularly seen at night from the airbase. It could all have so easily been blamed on some such accident from the bombers, so it was inconclusive to his parents at the end of the day. Only his mother would have seen the stain in their pants.

Dad is now in his mid seventies and went back to visit the site to see if there had been any re-growth in the woodland that was. He did find a small wood on the site, he was pleased to say, which he and his brothers had accidentally cleared for his granddad with the vary light. It must have been replanted and recovered over the years. He felt all the better for seeing it as he had not visited this site for many years, not wanting to visit the scene of the crime so to speak. It had worried him for years. He said he lost sleep over it for a long time afterwards.

It was the winter of the same year and dad was ten years old. He remembers going over to the air force base and it had been snowing hard and there was a good covering on the ground. He waited for the yanks to leave through the gates as they came off at the end of their shifts.

Dad and a couple of his brothers hid up and lay in wait for them to come out. As they went past he remembers throwing snowballs at some of them who took it with good grace and fun. Some of them were on bicycles and it was one of these men that he caught smack in the chops, as he put it. The airman skidded a long way trying to keep control of his bike. Meantime dad heard the cursing and turned and ran as fast as he could. He had to find some where to hide and quick. He knew he would near kill him if he could get hold of him. It seemed he'd thrown the snowball at the wrong man on this occasion.

Luckily close by there was a rabbit hutch, of all things, along with a resident rabbit. It was a bit cramped but he thought his life depended on it at the time. He had to stay there for quite a while, all curled up and cosy, nose to nose with a pet rabbit whilst he could hear the airman shouting and bawling out to him that he was going to have him when he got hold of him.

After a while it went quiet outside but he stayed a bit longer in the rabbit hutch just in case the airman was hanging around to catch him out. He said, *"thank God he never found me, I was nearly doing it in my trousers I was so scared!"*

BURNING RUBBER

It was a rusty and abandoned framework that dads' little brother Nidda (Edward) found. It was the chassis of an old car, which had been left abandoned in an overgrown corner of a field close to the army base. The engine was still on it though, although it didn't work. It had no windows, doors or a floor. In fact there was no bodywork whatsoever. He was so excited about it, as in those days if you had a car to run around in you were considered to be very upper class or a snob. All the ordinary folk had to make do with walking everywhere or you had two wheels on your bike and were thankful for it, whether it had tyres or not.

Nidda was it turned out, a bit of a natural at fixing up cars. He was only a youngster, when he had found this, probably no more than fourteen years old at the most. He was interested in how machinery worked and it took him a while through his early teens but he found out how to make the engine work and then got it going. He took some boards from the cowsheds to put in as a floor and went to the tip to find what he could to make some seating. He got himself an upturned box to sit on so he could control the steering, gears and brakes. Dad said he was so amazed that this rusty skeletal heap would ever move but it did and the boys all piled onboard, straight onto the makeshift floorboards that hung across it, untied or tethered. If it had been in these days they wouldn't have got twenty yards along the road as it didn't resemble anything remotely like a car other than it had four wheels and an engine with a steering wheel to drive it. Neither was there any other traffic as they pulled out of the farm driveway never looking left or right to see what was coming along. They rarely saw another car or vehicle about and they had complete right of way to themselves, never meeting anything to be a danger to anyone other than a cart horse with a cart or a very occasional Fordson, or Ferguson tractor which were rare anyway in those parts. Dad said he considers himself lucky to be alive still to this day, driving around at speeds as they did then, despite being shot at a number of times in his later life, which will appear a bit later on in his story.

Nidda would take his brothers around all the quiet roads around their home and drive for miles enjoying the view. They explored further afield discovering a new world miles out of their own known territory. There was so little traffic on the road even further away from home except for the horse and carts used by the farmers. The vehicle drove well despite its looks. They had many a number of trips in this open chassis of a car. He said *"it was a pity we didn't have the bodywork to go with it!"* No one else had a car that they knew of and all felt privileged to have had the experience of driving around in their youth, like young lords. Dad recalls he was proud of his little brother for what he had achieved with the car and then recalls another memory of his, about his brother, Nidda.

Nidda had a motorbike about the same time and it went like a rocket. It was an A.J.S 500. He acquired it very cheaply as it didn't work at the time. He got it going again quite quickly, even though it was old. The bike was made in 1929 or there-abouts. It was the fastest thing on two wheels at the time, they thought. He would take it to the fields around home to race it about, flat out.

Norwich Speedway was all the thing at the time and Nidda must have thought in his own mind that he was one of the team as he went round the fields at top speed, leaning into the bends as he gathered speed in his turns, his knee almost touching the ground in mid turn. On this one occasion barbed wire had been stretched across the field to keep cattle off the grass on one side of the field. He must have spotted it at the same time as all the boys, who shouted and screamed at him jumping up and down in their anxiety to alert him of the wires presence. He was too far away from them to hear the shouts of his brothers as he would be concentrating on just keeping on the bike and not scraping his knees. He narrowly missed out on a terrible accident that day as he showed his natural skill in avoiding it at the last second. In the meantime the boys were all doing it in their trousers again at the near miss. They loved each other and were very close, so much so that they didn't want to see him hurt. Mother had a lot of washing to do once again.

Nidda often went to the speedway on a Saturday night trying to always be in the audience on the bends in order to watch the bikers skid and crash where he could see them along with a lot of young hopefuls at the time. He would swear as he came in the door when he got home as the bikers nearly always crashed on some other corner away at the other end, where he couldn't see it.

Their Father was always supportive of them all if any of them showed an interest in boxing, as he was pretty good himself. Nidda had also taken to the sport like a natural when he was quite young and his father encouraged him to fight in local matches when he was ready. He would go to Norwich to train sometimes and to take part in organised bouts with boys of his own age range. And he was very good at it, having an especially good right hander.

It would seem the boys at school would see something in Nidda's face, and want to pick a fight with him. Dad said he had what you would call a miserable face at that time of his life.

He was generally a quiet young boy, but those boys who picked on him picked the wrong one to have a go at, as he could handle himself very well when it came to a scuffle.

One young man regularly had a bit of a go at Nida

verbally, in fact became more aggressive with it as time went on. He must have been looking for a fight hoping that one day he would get it.

One night they bumped into each other in the country road near to home.

Nidda wasn't about to take it any more and when words became heated the other youngster hit him with a bike lamp and Nidda laid him out right there in the road whilst dad looked on.

Dad pretended that he had nothing to do with his brother and was just merely an onlooker, which was just in case that anyone else was watching. It was none of his business after all, but he did not want to leave the boy lying out cold in the road, even if it was the middle of no-where and cars passed that way rarely.

Dad made the suggestion to his brother about moving him to the side of the road but his answer was *"leave the bastard where he is"* and so they did, leaving him to cool off as they turned their backs and walked home.

As dads' ability grew in being able to trap and shoot rabbits, and having more pocket money available, he decided he wanted to buy himself a new bicycle, to make life easier. He had saved up his money until he had about three pounds ten shillings when he saw an advert for a bike for sale. He went some way to get it and paid for it, bringing it home after trying it out.

It took about six months before he had any trouble with it even though it had some very hard use by him. He told me that one side of the handlebars fell off, so being as practical as he had become, he replaced it with a stick of approximately the same width and length. He said it was just as good as new.

It was another six months like this when one peddle fell of. Yet again he replaced the missing piece with another stick, but this didn't work quite so well and it soon broke off and he had to abandon the bike, as he couldn't use it again. He realised he couldn't use it anymore with just the one peddle.

In more recent times, he is now in his seventies, I have known that he has fixed things with a stick in much the same manner, continuing to function, helped along with the addition of a piece of blue or orange string from the bales which shows his ingenuity, albeit a little impractical. But it works for him usually even if it is only temporary. You will still find in his shed all sorts of things he has hanging up there which are held together with coloured string and twigs or sticks. He never was the engineer of the family. It would seem his little brothers had acquired all those engineering genetics and it had somehow bypassed him altogether. Some of his friends still call him "blue string" to this day. He still has a game bag of at least forty years which is still pulled out for use for hand feeding. It is held together with baling twine of various colours, with an old moth eaten hat stuffed into the bottom corner of the bag which the mice have chewed away at over the years. The hat is used to *"regulate"* the flow of corn seeping out as he walks along the woodland rides throwing wheat out along the woodland floor.

BACK ON THE FARM

It was the summer of 1945 and dad was just fourteen. His father had found him a job with horses on the farm nearby. The double summertime in those days was still being used to help the war effort, which meant that the clocks had been put back two hours instead of the usual one hour. Days seemed very long when you were out in the fields in the heat of the sun. This job was quite hard work in that you had to keep going. If you didn't take your own water or drink with you, you got nothing to drink all day; neither did the horses until they stopped work late in the evening. He only got a half hour break all day long, which he didn't think much of. Because it was double summertime it meant that it was quite late in the evening before it got dark so workdays were lengthened and everyone was expected to work them to the full. Work started at five thirty in the morning on this farm. It was light enough to see up to eleven at night.

While at work he pined to be out in the woods or down by the riverside but had a huge great horse to look after all day, along with the cart that went behind of course.

The job entailed loading up the carts with the sheaves of corn from the fields and taking them back fully loaded to the barns at the farm to be stored. The carts needed to be emptied by hand.

As the day got on the horses would tire and be more reluctant to walk away from their home at the farm. These were Shire horses. Dad said he would have to coax his horse to go to the other end of the field to collect the corn as it was further away each time and the outward journey was far slower than the homeward one. This horse would go along quite nicely on its return journey even if it were fully loaded. He supposes that the horse was hoping that this was its last journey of the day as it was not only thirsty but also hungry from its long day out in the hot sun. The horses weren't watered at all during the workday; they were worked for a full day without breaks except for the half hour the workers were allowed in the early afternoon.

As the evening progressed, his horse became a bit skittish and obviously had had enough, wanting to get back to the farm. It had been a long and hot day.

It was his first week working on the farm, and he took the horse back to the yard, where he had been shown how to back his horse up to the barn to unhitch the cart for the night. It would have then been time to feed her and give her a drink, but she had other ideas. She must have known that he was a beginner and that it probably took him longer to unhitch her from her cart.

There was a pond in the middle of the yard that the horses all made their own way to for a drink. It was at this time that the rest of their tackle would normally be removed as they drank their fill of water. On his return there must have been between twelve and fifteen huge carthorses milling around the pond eating and drinking. All were allowed to walk free as they were usually too tired to run about at the end if the day and more interested in filling their stomachs and quenching their thirst.

Dads' horse was impatient, having other ideas, deciding that she was not going to wait for him to unhitch her cart fully, and so she bolted.

She had the shafts of the cart still attached to her along with the two front wheels, but still had all the trimmings poking out and crashing into the barn taking some of it with her in her haste to get away. She ran off towards the pond at full gallop, bits flying about everywhere. She was eventually seen to be standing knee deep in the middle of the pond with only the shafts still attached drinking happily. My father said he didn't know what to do when she broke loose and went and hid as quickly as he could behind the barn, only coming out when he felt it safe to do so.

The boss was alerted by all the noise and had come out to shout at him for letting the horse get the better of him. He was angry about the damage to his barn and to his cart, which was in bits. Shouting loudly as he walked about the yard looking to find dad, who was nowhere to be seen, telling him that he would give him a good hiding for what had happened when he got hold of him. Suddenly his father appeared, walking across the farmyard having heard what had been said. His reply to the boss was, *"You will have to give me one first!"*

Needless to say that the farmer had to let the matter drop, as he knew of his father's ability to have a fight in the ring and would not take his chances. It turned out that dad only got the one telling off, from a distance. Creeping out of hiding behind the barn having heard the exchange with the two men, the matter was dropped.

It was after this episode he decided he did not want to continue working with the horses as he missed the freedom of being out in the countryside too much. His father helped find him some other work, getting a few odd jobs helping the keepers on the estates instead. This is what he wanted to do for a living he decided, as he was happiest when in this environment.

As dad grew up at Salhouse with the family he had been encouraged to work on the estates to earn a bit of money with his father and uncles. He remembers he would get paid a shilling to go beating on the shooting estates as a young boy in the autumn and winter. He and his father and brothers would go regularly on most days of the week and he continued to do this all throughout his youth. He helped out the keepers when they needed the help and went round the farms to work alongside his father in the fields at other times, doing whatever was needed on the day, be it planting up or ploughing, weeding or harvesting.

When he was out around the fields he continued to set traps and snares and net the rabbits to make a bit of money sometimes getting a badger or fox for their skins. He would catch a few moles for their skins as he would get five or sometimes sixpence a time for a good one. If he were lucky he would sometimes get a coypu and skin it, as it was sought after by the local furriers in Norwich. He learnt that the skins had to be stretched out in the right way by using nails in the correct places. This was an art in itself and he had made a few mistakes in his time, and knew that the furriers would not pay as much for an imperfect skin. There had to be no bullet holes in it or tears. There was only one way and that was the right way.

Horace Friend Ltd, the furrier to whom he sent on his skins to, had been in Wisbech Cambridgeshire since

1860 and not only took all the fox, badger, stoat, coypu, rabbit, cat and mole skins, but they also took Jay wings and starling feathers and good quality pheasant tails, along with anything else that had interest such as mane and tail hair. So there was plenty of scope for a youngster to make a little extra cash if he saw the opportunity.

It was a well known fact in those days that all the farm workers as well as the keepers would set a few snares as they went about the fields to work. It all helped when it came to harvest time as in those days you would only get about half a ton of corn to each acre, but nowadays the farmers will often as not get four and a quarter tons to the acre. This shows how much of a nuisance the rabbits were then and how efficient the modern day farmers' methods are today.

He decided about this time he wanted to get himself a twelve-bore shotgun. He had already saved up and bought himself a .22 rifle and a four-ten as well as a number of airguns that his younger brothers would often borrow if they had the ammunition. The boys would get their complete egg collections and sell them on for a bit of cash to help pay for the guns or the pellets they needed to use them. They also sold their card collections to make up any shortfall if it was needed. The boys could always look out for more eggs as there were plenty of nests around. Dad was fifteen at the time and had only shot with other peoples twelve bores and wanted to own one of his own. It was the next natural stage.

Once again he saved all that he could and when he considered it enough he looked and asked around to find one for sale. He saw an advert and arranged to go and see the gun a young man had advertised locally. He was taken into the back garden to try it out. He was handed the gun to load and fire.

Right there and then he saw a sparrow get up and fly across the garden from the fence, looking as though it would land on the ferret hut across the other side of the garden.

He lifted the gun and fired at it, *"blowing it into hundreds of pieces"*. He made the instant decision and told the young man, *"Yes, I'll take it!"*

Of a night time he would take himself off to get a few pheasants. Of course it was not his first time at poaching and he would never like to admit it even to this day. He had come to realise that he knew he could have what he wanted out in the fields, day or night. He was so proud of his achievements and the few pheasants hanging in the larder on his return. He would creep upstairs to the bedroom he still shared with his brothers in the early hours of the morning whispering loudly as he entered the room *"Are you awake?"* It was always a rather loud stage whisper as he always wanted to recount his nights' activities, having an audience to perform to, in his younger brothers.

He sometimes got up very early in the morning to go around the keepers' traps and snares and reset all those he had taken the rabbits from. It would seem that the keepers knew very little of his night time and early morning forays as he was so good at resetting the traps again. He sold on all his ill gotten gains to the locals and to anyone who had asked him.

It was about this time that the Ministry of Agriculture decided to add dressings to the seeds the farmers planted. This was to help deter the pigeons and birds that fed on them at planting time. The seed was not buried as deep as it is today, a lot would have been left on the surface for the birds to pick at, as farming methods were not as efficient in those years.

Taking his new gun to go and shoot the pigeons coming in over the fields he remembers seeing a blue and grey carpet of pigeons lying there, having died after eating the dressed seeds. There were hundreds if not thousands of them and they would regularly be found like that on the fields that had been replanted. No one else seemed to bother about it all but it upset him as the birds had no chance of survival and it seemed like mass murder as there were thousands of birds that were killed in a short space of time. The seeds are still dressed today but the authorities must have realised the devastation that was caused and changed the formula to lessen the fatalities.

It wasn't so long after this that myxamatosis was introduced to keep the rabbit population down. It killed off much of the rabbit population in Great Britain, taking many years for them to get back to an accepted level of population, never to be the same as it once was.

GAMEKEEPER AT LAST

When he was seventeen he began to think of his own career, knowing what he wanted to achieve and started to ask about if there were any jobs going in the area. He was put in touch with the head keeper Bill Bowman on the estate at Hornby Castle, up in Lancashire. Sir Harold Parkinson owned the estate, and the job was described as a boy keeper's job.

This was the opening he had been looking for; he knew he needed the experience in all keepering aspects. It would also bring him in a proper wage he had not had previously. This was two pounds a week, something he had previously had to work hard at, getting rabbits every day to get that amount. The money wasn't as important as he knew he would be doing what he loved most and getting paid for it was a bonus. His aim was to become a head keeper himself in the future, but he needed to learn the skills by working on different estates, as each one was different. Each had its own ways and the more experience he got the better he would learn.

The Hornby estate was trying to get back to something near what it had been before the war and they wanted to employ more keepers to get it there. It had once been a very good and thriving shoot, but all the keepers had been called up for duties in the forces and it was left in the care of Bill Bowman to look after as best he could.

Dad knew that he had the experience of rearing and feeding back home in Norfolk and knew that he would be capable of doing the job at Hornby. He knew what was expected of him and wanted to learn more about it all from the right man.

He applied for the job and went up for his interview. He liked Mr Bowman on sight and he recalls that he stood looking over the bridge at Hornby at the end of the day, facing the castle in its perfect backdrop setting. He stood in awe alongside the keeper who just pointed, both taking in the wonderful sight of the trees, castle and landscape in the glorious sunset which filled their view. Both were appreciative of this wonderful beauty spot and stood in silence to admire it.

Bill Bowman had taken up dads' references having spoken to someone back at home before he got there. It was established that he had come from a very good country family and was excellent at rabbiting, trapping and shooting as he had proclaimed at his interview. He had done some rearing with the broody hens too and talked readily of his previous experiences. Hearing him talk about what he had done in boyhood, Bill Bowman would have known he was a good hard working, keen country boy, and be right for the job.

Mr Bowman knew that he could make good use of dads' skills as they were overrun with rabbits and dad had quite a bit of experience with game, not only shooting it but also rearing and feeding. He was offered the job at the end of the interview on the day and went home to tell the family. He was just seventeen.

Another young man was also interviewed about the same week, for another position of under keeper and was taken on to start his job at the same time.

Mr Bowman had told him that he would arrange for somewhere for dad to lodge, close to work, and on arrival he was sent to the village of Wray, situated on the estate grounds. He was given an address in the village that were expecting him and took in lodgers who worked for the estate.

Dad says he had never lived in a village ever before and that this felt a bit strange to him. He had never had to work out a number or name of a house as his family home in Norfolk was the only one in the fields and stood out on its own. He could have found his family home in the dark in the fields but here if you turned him round twice in the villages and towns he wouldn't know where on Earth he was.

His landlord and landlady Mr and Mrs Sedgewick were a good country family and knew and understood the working practices of the keepers on the estate. Dad recalls he had to pay one pound and ten shillings for his keep to the family which meant he had a whole ten shillings left over for himself. Nowadays that would be the equivalent of fifty pence. He didn't drink or smoke and said he felt quite wealthy then, never having that much money regularly for himself in his life.

He had a cooked breakfast early every morning and when he got in of an evening was given another good meal. He said that because he had walked for so many miles during the daytime over the hills to the woods he was often feeling starving hungry. When he had been given his meal of an evening, which he said was so good that he could eat it again; Mrs Sedgewick would give the dogs the leftovers and never asked him if he wanted anymore. He was young and not so forward or courageous enough to ask if he could have some more, and he remembers that if she wasn't around he would have fought the dog for its meal, he was that hungry all the time. He needed good food to keep his strength and stamina up, as he was still a growing lad of seventeen.

One of dads' first jobs he had to do most mornings at eight a.m as a boy keeper was to chop the kindling for the head keepers' wife and to keep a wood pile of cut logs in readiness for their fires. He would have to clean out the dogs kennels as well every morning on his arrival at the head keepers' cottage. This was the time that the head keeper gave him his instructions for the day. He would then have to often walk miles over the two and a half thousand acre estate to the woods for feeding or whatever was needed that day. He had no complaints however as he loved the job and said he would have done it for no pay if it was necessary. However, as part of his pay he was also given a good suit to wear and if he had a wife at home he would have been given some coal for the home fires as well.

As it turned out most of the village were accepting of the estate and its shoots and the gamekeepers who worked there. All the locals seemed to understand the running of it, as he found out over the following weeks.

On his first day at work when he came back to the village in the evening he forgot which house he was lodging at. The first person he saw walking towards him down the street was a young, vibrant red headed woman of about the same age as he. She was carrying a bucket of fresh pigs' blood down to a neighbours' house for him to make black puddings with. He recalls the light tapping noise as her wooden clogs touched against the cobbles of the road as she walked. Dad stopped her to ask if she knew of his landlady as he was lost and couldn't remember which door to knock on or where he was staying. He explained he was new to the village. She took him to his lodging house and it turned out that it was only six doors away from her own home.

He didn't know it then but this bright red headed woman would in the future become his wife and my mother. Her name was Margaret Joan Clarkson and she had been born not far from the village of Wray and had lived and gone to the local village school there. She and her family lived at Doreen Cottage in the village.

After this first time, he saw her regularly on his way out to work and of an evening when he had finished work for the day. It was meant to be and soon he met up with the whole of the family, the parents, William Robert and Margaret Anne Clarkson and younger sister, Doreen and younger brother Bill, all of whom were interested in him although a little suspicious of this long haired young man who spoke with a very broad Norfolk accent.

He liked her mother, who was a Cumbrian woman and who spoke with an awful lot of thee's and thou's in her chatter to him. It took a long time to understand her speech but he got to understand her after a while. It also helped as the head keeper on the estate was a Cumbrian man so allowing a little more practice of hearing the dialect during his working day.

Bill Bowman was about seventy even then, finding comfort in being able to talk in his own dialect in the same village with someone who understood him thoroughly, he would often call in to see Joan's mother for a cup of tea. This also meant that her mother knew all about his job and what it entailed.

Her mother and father kept pigs and hens, so having a plentiful supply of ham, bacon and eggs for the family and to those who had sent round their vegetable peelings and scraps for the animals. They also grew their own vegetables and had a grape vine up the wall of the warmer side of the house. The family would look out for those around them and bartered off any excess they had.

They had the only good bathroom in the village, with a proper bath and hot running water to it supplied by a copper that was heated by fire. The army would ask my grandmother to use the facilities for the army officers, when they were in the area. They would apparently bring their own soap with them and leave what they hadn't used behind when they had finished with it. Soap was in short supply during the war years, as was hot running water for the bath. My mother told me that she made a few more friends when it became known that they had a bath and hot water and they would ask if they could have a hot bath when they came round to visit.

Dad was taken around the village and introduced to some more of her family. Her fathers' sister, Aunty Ruth and Uncle Jack Whittam lived along the main street of Wray village. One of her grannies had lived in the same village in a tiny two up two down terraced house along the main street, bringing up a houseful of children. Some of these had moved on and out of the village as they grew up, but a few stayed on and brought up their families. The villagers were a close knit community and looked out for each other wherever they could.

There were a number of other families whom she had grown up and gone to school with. Joan Holroyd was her best friend throughout their school years and lived in the village. There were also the Robinson, Parker, Sedgewick and Kenyon families. All became known to my dad as he began to mix with the teenagers of the village of an evening or when he had some free time from his job.

There was a small shop and a post office along with a small library and a coal merchant's yard in the village. Over the years there had also been a clog maker and a workshop that made nails.

My mother told me that her uncle had a shop in those days in Lancaster, where he would get the family in to do a fitting and make all their clogs himself.

In the basement of Doreen Cottage, mum's family home, there had once been a hat maker's workshop where they made top hats, and all that remained were the benches where her father now cut up the butchered pigs and cured the bacon.

For many years there had been a series of open cast coal mines run by some of the locals in various locations close to the village. My mother told me her father and his family had worked there and been heavily involved in the work at these sites throughout the previous years. It was at this time run by the Robinson family and all the local coal was delivered by their own carts and eventually Lorries from their yard at the side of their home.

The small but busy village hall was also where you went of a Saturday night to see the latest film and where many of the children and teenagers met up. Wall's ice cream, cylindrically sliced and wrapped in paper was served up at the interval of the films. It was later on that Italian ice cream became more of a treat for the youngsters of the village.

The local swimming pool was up behind the village. The river which cut through and round the edges of the village had deeper pools cut naturally into the huge rocks just down from a quarry. There was one particular spot which was wide and deep enough to do a decent length for those who were serious enough to have a go at it. It was where the youngsters gathered to swim on the warmer days and was a popular spot for many of the villagers who were hardy enough to swim in the fresh cool waters of the northern river which came down from the high dales of Lancashire.

ABSENCE MAKES THE HEART GROW FONDER

It was during their courtship that dad would often take my mother with him when he went to work. He told me she was very patient with him as he often had to see her whilst he worked. She would walk along with him no matter how many miles he had to go in order to see to his traps and snares and reset them again. They would roam the estate and meet up sometimes with other local teenagers and go on to the pictures occasionally.

On one such meander across the fields towards their destination, my mother suddenly realised there was usually a bull in this particular field. She was dressed particularly well this day and had a good pair of fashionable shoes on. My father looked out into the field and told her there was no bull there today. He had decided on his way out to take this detour to check on a few snares and told my mother she would be safe to walk across the field and he would meet her on the other side when he had attended to his work, which would only take a few minutes to complete. He told her she would tear her dress and get untidy if she came through the hedges and into the woods and said it would be quicker for her to go straight across the fields.

She stepped into the field and started to make her way across when she realised she was no longer alone. At the other end of the field she saw the bull come running over towards her at speed. By this time she was in the middle of the field and had to make a run for it. She panicked and ran for all she was worth just making it to the gate the other end as the angry bull caught up with her.

My father appeared around from the hedge at the side of the gate, laughing to see her breathless as she bolted over it.

He told me he knew the bull was there somewhere, but it wasn't in sight and must have been in a dip as he looked over the field. *"It was just unlucky the bull looked up when he did!"* He told me *"it was a very nasty natured bull and I wouldn't personally have gone through that field if I had seen it!"*

My mother was upset with him. All he could do was laugh at how she had run so fast. He still smiles with a cheeky grin to this day at the memory of it.

He told me of an incident which wiped the smile off his face though as it was so serious, although he said it was unintentional.

My grandmother loved her cat very dearly and one day it went missing. She'd had the cat for a number of years and it had never strayed too far away from home before, always coming back home of a night. There had been a lot of cats wandering off and going missing within a few months and she thought she might have found the solution to the problem.

One evening as dad arrived home, she went round to his lodging house to confront him about all the cats in the village going missing. She asked him outright if he was the cause and he flatly denied it all to her, promising quite faithfully that it was nothing to do with him. She warned him that if she found out any different she would not allow him to see her daughter ever again.

She was stood, he recalls, with her back to the shed door, at the rear of the property of his lodging house, and if she had gone through that particular door she would have found the skin of her pet cat stretched and nailed out in a nice flat piece on the back of the wooden door, drying in readiness to send to the furriers, Horace Friend. He knew by the description she had given him that it was nailed out alongside skins of moles, weasels and stoats. He said he got one shilling and sixpence for each cat skin, which was very little in today's equivalent of seven and a half pence. He did it because it made him a bit more money regularly. Surrounding it on all the other walls of the shed were the furry remains of the rest of the village cats that had also gone missing. He told me that it was a perk of the job to get a few shillings extra a week for skins and after all a cat was just another poacher to him. There were too many of them about anyway.

It wasn't illegal to shoot a marauding cat in those days as they could kill a large number of young pheasant chicks and smaller birds. They would appear every day if they were local and the numbers of kills would soon total up if they weren't stopped.

He said if she had found this out right there and then, I and my brothers and sisters would not have been born as she would have had his guts for garters, she was so fired up about it. He couldn't have told her the truth even if he wanted to at this stage. It was just unlucky that her cat had been found in the woods along with the others as he said it was never intentional, never wanting to upset her or her daughter. If he had known it was her cat he would not have done what he did.

He said it took him a long time to admit the truth to my mother later on, even though he thought she had guessed it was he, as all the family were looking for the cat for a long time after it went missing. He says they may have all suspected him, but there was no proof, even though they knew the ways of a gamekeeper.

He also said that over a period of time he got a lot of money for the skins of foxes, badgers and cats he sent away, along with the mole and otter skins, as he needed a bit more cash as his social life was starting to take off. He said at the time he saw no wrong in it as it was something he had done all his life and there just happened to be lots of nice looking cats about in the village. He explained cats would go out onto the estate which surrounded the village and catch a pheasant to eat, much the same as the cats had done when back in Norfolk. He said it was natural for him to kill the predators and it was always a bonus to get money for the skins.

Douglas Watker, one of dads' friends from home in Norfolk whom he had gone through school with in his teens, came up to visit him for a week or two. Douglas was also a good country boy who enjoyed the same interests as my father and they had got on well. They had kept in touch when he moved away to his new job. It was a small village and my dad and his friend were soon chatting to the other young local teenagers. Douglas met one of my mothers' friends', Hillary Robinson, a young girl from the same village of Wray. The two liked one another and Douglas became a regular visitor to the village and the couple eventually married.

My grandfather was also interested in dads' daily activities and when he got to know him a little better he would call round to his lodgings of an evening and want to hear of the day's activities. The landlord was also as keen as he and the pair of them would question him about what he had seen and done of an evening if he was in.

My grandfather was interested enough to go out with him when he went to get rabbits and would also be keen enough to go along on a days rough shooting as well. They would take the head keepers dogs if they needed them for picking up or to flush out the rabbits wherever they went. Grandfather got on very well with my dad and he would always ask to go along of a night time, long netting for rabbits. He was a lorry driver by day and he must have enjoyed the change as he loved the countryside as well as anyone else.

There was one fly in the ointment at the beginning of his time at the Hornby estate in that the other young man that had been employed as under keeper at the same time was a bit of a cheat. He would go round dads' traps and remove his rabbits, stoats and weasels, claiming them as his own to the head keeper.

This had to be sorted out pretty quickly and dad got him up against a wall one day and threatened him. The young man apparently never did it again. His job did not last very long after that, obviously he couldn't cope as well in the job as he had originally said he could and left.

Not everyone is cut out for this kind of life and most people find that the keenness leaves them after a while and the job becomes a bore.

Dad remembers he had a young boy from the village who would follow him around. His name was Colin Hilton and he would help the keepers out whenever he could after school and at weekends. He was so keen. His granddad was Bill Bowman, the head keeper so it must have been in the blood with him as well. When dad eventually left this estate, Colin became a full time keeper and as far as he knows is still there today.

He does recall as a boy, Colin shot a white owl on the estate and dad wasn't happy with him about it. He remembers him creeping up behind the bushes near to where he was working, thinking he was going to shoot a rabbit but shot the owl instead. He felt the need as a lot of youngsters do, in killing the slightly different species when they see them. This one met its fate only because of its colour.

Dad pointed out to me that a barn owl which is white does not kill pheasants, so is not a threat for the keepers and the one that was shot, was not a barn owl, but a different breed altogether.

This was the forties; owls were plentiful in this area

and would pick off the young pheasant chicks when they were out in the fields. He would use pole traps to get a few every week as these methods were legal up until the early fifties. It was part of dads' job to kill them off, as they were such a nuisance and there were so many of them. Most of these were tawny owls. He recalls telling his boss about an unusual small owl he had seen up on the edges of the estate. He was told to shoot it as it was the only way to see it in those days and he brought it back to show Bill who recognised a species he had not seen in that area ever before as they had only been known to live a lot further south of the country.

Bill Bowman always wanted to know what dad had seen when he had been out on the estate. There were a large number of red squirrels on the estate which he was told to shoot, as there were so many at that time. There were also a lot of stoats he recalls which needed trapping as they had become a nuisance in their numbers during the breading season. They would sneak up and eat a lot of the wild eggs in the nests so it was important to cull as many as he could.

Up along the back of the village there was a place called Backsbottom in which he remembers there were a lot of otters. He would go after them because of their skins. This site was an old quarry which probably had not been worked for a hundred years before. The indentations in the stones were like caves going deep into the earth where ore had been dug out and the workmen had once mined. The otters lived deep in these fissures as there was water all around. It was a beautiful spot with rock pools and overhanging greenery. Dad said that he would walk in as far as he could until he couldn't stand upright anymore. He would then walk in bowed over at the waist until he couldn't carry on upright any further. He said that he would lie down in the water so he could follow the otter's footprints as far in as he could see, but said he didn't see as many footprints going in the other direction. He just knew there were quite a few otters around and he occasionally would trap or shoot one in that area. He would be able to get two pounds and five shillings for each skin up until the early forties so it was worth a try when he had the time to go and look. It was a lot of money in those days. He said he wouldn't dream of going after otters these days.

More often than not though he would get a badger as well as there were a lot of them about on that estate and they caused more damage in the woods than the otters, also fetching a good price.

Dad learned a lot from Bill Bowman on the estate that summer and they reared some of their own pheasants for the first time since the war. They had the broody hens in rows of sitting boxes fifteen inches square each on the fields sitting on eighteen eggs per hen. When they were hatched out they would be put into the coops that were bigger. They were approximately two feet six square. Later on they took them to the pens they had built down the woods and released them into the wild. This was the first season for a number of years hatching the eggs as it used to be. Bill Bowman and dad worked together well and dad proved to him that he knew what he was doing whilst learning more about this area from him. As part of the estate was moorland on which they had some grouse, this became part of the shoot.

Of course the owner of the estate, Sir Harold Parkinson

had arranged a full shooting season that autumn because of the success of the hatch, all being it not as huge as it once had been before wartime years.

Whilst out and about working on the estate he recalls seeing a ten shilling note on the ground and picked it up. On seeing the head keeper he told him what he had found, handing it over. The problem was that it was a couple of days after pay day and he couldn't find his own ten shilling note on reaching home that night, not realising that it was his own money he was handing over. He had to go back to the head keepers' house to explain himself and ask for it back.

They went on to have a second good year on the estate with the hatching and rearing culminating in another very successful shoot for the owner.

Towards the end of the second year, dad heard of another job over in Brough, Beverly, Yorkshire. He still felt he needed new experiences and the only way of getting this was by changing his job to other estates. On each shoot there were slight differences that only by doing the job could he learn. He had been over the moors shooting and trapping rabbits with some of the locals on quite a number of occasions during the time that he worked at Hornby Castle. He would go with the local policeman and the butcher shooting grouse on these moors, but having seen more whilst he was out for the day shooting the grouse, he felt enticed further onto the moors by the number of rabbits that bred very happily. They were everywhere he looked on the estate at Beverly and when he was taken on as the third keeper, he was in his natural element. He was never happier in those days than when out rabbiting.

He was given a gross (144) of snares and a gross of gin traps and told to get as many rabbits as he could.

In the forties he used the big gin traps as they were considered to be very good as you could hide them very well. They are not used today but they were the best traps of their day he told me and couldn't be beaten.

He had very well trained Labrador dogs for picking up from the estate kennels and he recalls going along the railway tracks on the sides of the banks where he could shoot rabbits all day long as they appeared out of their holes in the sun. Ferrets were put down the holes to bolt them out. The dogs would know only to go after an injured rabbit that was still on the move and leave the rest to be picked up later.

At the end of the day, dad told me he would take a pony and trap or the sledge to collect the huge amount of rabbits he had got in that days work. Whilst he was out he would set traps and snares as well. All these traps and snares needed to be checked regularly. It was so cold and frosty in the early mornings and at night when he went out he would have sore hands from opening the traps and setting them again. The sores on his hands would split open and bleed and be painful to use. He was so keen to go out he never let the sores stop him doing what he loved to do, getting excited because he said that the numbers never seemed to go down. He would see just as many rabbits about the next morning as there had been on the previous day.

Dad said that he did do all the work that was needed as a young boy keeper throughout the keeper's year with the pheasants, but just seems to remember all the shooting he did, on this particular estate. He was in his natural element and did as much rabbitting as he has ever done up until that point in his life.

He told me that for no reason that he can ever think of, his boss called him Jimmy all the time that he was working there, and never called him George, ever. He accepted it in good faith but to this day, never found out the reason why.

He lodged with the head keeper and his wife so he was on the estate most of the time he worked there.

He and my mother by this time had become engaged to be married and they did not see enough of each other, as they would have liked.

Dad was kept so busy on the estate what with the normal duties of a young boy keeper, like chopping firewood and piling it up at the doorway, as well as cutting all the kindling. He had to clean out the dog kennels every morning before carrying on with his normal duties which would be often to walk miles to the woods for feeding, once the young pheasant chicks had been put out into the woods in the summer. He would often take one of the dogs with him on his rounds as they were always keen for a walk about and didn't get as much work in the summer. He would use them for picking up when he took his gun for rabbiting. A keeper's day is very long and there are few days off as the birds need to be fed and watered every day without fail. Someone else has to be able to do the work if a day off is needed and all keepers need to be dedicated to their job and all of its requirements, twenty-four seven, all year round.

During this time, on one occasion, his younger brother Herbert came up to stay for a week or two during the summer to see him. He went around with him shooting and netting the rabbits and generally helped out with his daily routine. He tells me they were up and out on the moors shooting one day when they spotted a silver disc moving along in the sky. It had caught their attention as it was quite low but gave off no noise. It moved about quite slowly, changing its shape and seemed to hover as if waiting for them to catch up a little as they ran after it over the moorland. It apparently whisked off at high speed eventually. They had given chase for a mile or so before it disappeared from view. Of course they wondered what it may have been as they had never seen anything like it before or since. Both young men had been fascinated by it thinking it must be some new craft, but in later years they realised it must have been a UFO. They carried on with their shooting as if nothing had happened. Apparently you see all sorts when out in the countryside.

Up until then the young pheasants had been a little nearer to the keepers' cottage so they could be tended night and day. The chicks had the broody hens to watch over them whilst they grew up. At night they would go back under the hens to be sat on nice safe and warm until morning. The young pheasant chicks would still go to the calls of the hens for up to five or six weeks cuddling up to her where they could. After this time they would naturally try to get up to roost out of harms way. The hens still had to be fed and watered though and let out of their coops each morning to empty themselves and have a bit of a stretch. The young chicks would go wandering around the coops and the local surrounding field, mixing with all the other young poults.

Meat would have to be ground up for the young growing chicks feed every day, usually rabbit, and cooked up over a fire outside the huts on the edges of the rearing field. It was the head keepers' job to get the right mix of ingredients. The cooked meat was mixed with other fine grains and seeds, along with eggs, to be fed to the young pheasant chicks to ensure their health and growth. Dad said even he was often hungry, and would taste the mix, it was so good.

It was still double summer time even then and the

days were very long for the keepers. They would all have to be up and out in the rearing fields by four thirty in the morning, although they would often take it in turns for the earlier shifts. The birds were opened up at six o'clock and had their first feed and water. Next it was eleven in the morning, then again at four with a final session at seven at night. Often it wasn't dark until eleven at night and the chicks would be called by the mothers as the light was fading.

The keepers would put the covers over the front of the coops as it got dark in the fields to give extra protection from the predators like the foxes and owls that came out to feed at night. The keeper would have to creep up quietly from behind the individual coops, after the hen had called her brood under her for the night. Each of the chicks knew the clucking and calling of their own foster mother and always went back to her even if they had strayed on the field and been amongst the other hundreds of youngsters all day.

When he wasn't feeding and watering his pheasants in the woods, which were miles away from anywhere, dad would be trapping and shooting the vermin on the estate. Most of the vermin is unseen out in the countryside to the average person but in these days there were masses that had to be dealt with not only by the keepers but also the farmers. There were no other controls to deal with it. The only defence that a keeper had was to set tunnel traps, which were four inch rabbit traps set into the natural runs or even artificial tunnels along the normal thoroughfares of the ground vermin. It was in this way that stoats and weasels would be caught. They were very fast and mostly unseen in the woods. If they were left unchecked they would breed very quickly. They would silently creep up on a nesting pheasant or partridge and steal its eggs sometimes even as it sat there on the nest. They can burrow in underneath the nests and sneak in from beneath. Dad said that he once found a nest a family of stoats had deserted in an old rabbit earth. In it there were over fifty pheasant and partridge eggs in storage, having been taken by them from the nests in the wild.

There is an old saying that a trap never ate anything, it never minded waiting, and it was always at work when the keeper was asleep.

He says that it never worried him how far he had to walk and that many times he got lost and couldn't remember where he was, not recognising his surroundings. He said that he would carry on walking until he eventually would see slightly more familiar surroundings and make his way back towards home of an evening. He also knew where the sun was in the sky and which direction it would be in throughout the times of the day, so could always get some sort of bearing. It was rare to meet anyone out walking as it was private land and well known to be a shooting estate. It was far away from the normal footpaths the public followed when out for walks in the countryside.

He was usually carrying traps and a gun, and on his way home would pick out the rabbits he had got in the snares the previous day as he came across them. Sometimes he had set them only a few hours earlier that day.

When he went out intentionally to get the rabbits he would take along the estate pony and trap as well as a dog so as to carry the huge numbers that he got. If he was lucky he would get a few pence for the rabbits that he killed, and his immediate boss the head keeper did a deal with him about how much money he could have out of the sale of them. He was very keen to take them off him as he was making money himself, from the butchers that took them away. They settled on twopence for each rabbit but as it turned out dad got so many that he eventually only gave him a set amount of ten shillings a week. This didn't cover the cost of even a penny each sometimes, but it kept dad happy, knowing it didn't matter how many he got and he said that he would have done it for nothing, he so enjoyed himself being out there every day and doing what he most wanted to do.

Having rarely seen my mother, Joan in this year really did make the heart grow fonder. He decided that he could not stand being without her any longer and started to make plans to marry her and find a job with a house so they could be together. He told me that he could have got a house up close to his job at the time but thought it would be better to move on to another keepering job altogether and start again.

AND NOW THERE WERE TWO

Dad had started to save what he could from his bit of extra from the rabbits and from any vermin that he had got like the badger or fox skins.

At the same time my mother was also planning her escape from home and saved all that she could put aside for her new life.

My mother was a mill worker who worked on the looms in Wenning Silk Mills in High Bentham, a few miles from her home in Wray. Her income had become a large part of the household funding to keep the family and she had always given away all of her wages to her mother without too many questions up until now. She worked long hours and ran up to six looms in the factory at once, which in those days was a skill in itself. They paid her well for it, more so than most of the men who went out to work hard physical labour all day from the village.

In one of her diaries of that time she wrote down her pay for the days of the piece work that she worked on the looms. On some weeks she earned over ten pounds and five shillings, but normally it would be around seven pounds and ten shillings as a basic rate. The more looms she ran the higher her take home pay would be. A bonus was given out twice yearly, in the summer and at Christmas time depending on how much you had done.

In mums' case it was at least an extra pound and ten shillings a week which soon mounted up.

However, now that the couple had decided that it was time to plan their own lives, it became a difficult choice even though it was necessary to withhold some of her pay each week.

Before she got home she would use some of it to buy small items for her bottom drawer, so to speak. If it was already spent then her mother could not have it, and mum decided that her needs were just as great as her families. She had been good for a number of years in handing over the cash and it was now her turn to take some of what she had earned. Her family had done well out of her until now. She had provided for her family since she had been fourteen when she began working at the mill and they had all lived well in those five years. She knew that her own mother would miss the money she brought in and her mother did not want to encourage her to leave and marry my father as it would change everything.

By the time she got the call from my dad in Brough, Beverly to meet him at Leeds station she had enough saved to make a new start with him. She had saved about a hundred pounds, which in those days was a lot.

Dad said if she could not get away to the station to meet him on the day he had arranged to meet her, he would come and get her himself.

She had to arrange for a ration book and an identity card to be put in her name in readiness for her departure, which she did.

Mum told her boss about what she intended to do, telling him that her mother did not approve of her relationship with my dad; she wanted to marry him and as she was only eighteen, needed her parents' permission to marry at that time, so in effect they would have to run away to marry, to elope.

She knew her mother did not think my father would be good enough to marry her but she had fallen in love with him despite whatever her mother thought. Both of them were only nineteen years old at this time.

Her factory manager felt for her, as she was a good woman and had been a well thought of and steady employee for quite some time with him. When asked for a reference from him he readily gave her one, along with her wages up to date on the day of her departure. He told her he would give her a lift to the station and if she gave him an address he would work out all her back pay, in bonuses which by this time had amounted to quite a few pounds, telling her he would send it on. She gave him my fathers' home address at Salhouse and apparently he was as good as his word and did just that a couple of months later.

The couple met up at Leeds station and dad took her home to meet the family in Salhouse, Norfolk.

It was a bit of a shock to my mother as to how they all managed, as at home they had a bath with running hot and cold water and a flush toilet, albeit the only one in the village, and her mother was a good cook, having worked in service in a big country house before she married as had her own mother before her.

There were so many boys running around and not all of them were as accepting of her presence as they could be. She tried to show and teach my dads' mother a few things where she could in regard to cooking a slightly different menu while she was there, so as to help out in the house on a day-to-day basis. She was a natural country cook herself learning from her own mother and grandmother as well as having had good food prepared for her all her life. This was a bit of a culture shock.

After a few weeks she had found a job at Wroxham Broads Hotel as a chambermaid and waitress.

She worked there for a while and when she got home after a long days shift she found it difficult to cope with the complexities of a huge family of boys. She said that at least one of the brothers decided he did not like her and started making life a little difficult for the couple. The youngest two, Hado and Willy would follow them around wherever they went and it felt that they were spying on them, leaving them very little time to themselves.

Mum decided she would go and live in the local YMCA for a while. It was while she was there she found a job in a mill similar to the one that she had previously worked in, in Lancashire. It was a silk mill in Norwich and she had to look after only two looms here, which, they seemed to think was a very clever thing to do. She found this easy as she had worked and looked after six before.

Meanwhile my father was on the look out for a job as a keeper that would also have a house to go with it.

They arranged to marry at the local church, Thorpe St Andrews in Salhouse and the bans were read. My mother wrote to her parents to let them know the wedding had been arranged but they declined the offer to attend on the day. It was a simple ceremony and very few attended, except mums' closest friend Joan Holroyd who was Matron of Honour and Mr and Mrs Sedgewick from Wray.

It was dads' brother-in-law Peter Sturman, who gave my mother away on the big day. She had found a friend in him during her stay in Norfolk and he very kindly came to the rescue when her own father did not appear on the day of her wedding. It was November the 19th 1950.

Some of dads' family attended the wedding but his little brothers were very reluctant to go. They would much rather have been out with their airguns getting a few birds out in the woods. Each of them refused quite heartily and had to be persuaded to come along. It was only after lengthy discussions that they agreed, as long as they could bring along their guns to the wedding ceremony. It was that or nothing at all. So that's exactly what they did. It was truly an unusual shotgun wedding!

Afterwards there was a wedding breakfast to attend where they had sandwiches, trifle, and a wedding cake which mum paid three pounds for. At this time there was still rationing and mum had saved up all she could out of it, to go towards the meal.

She records in her diary it cost her a total of twenty seven pounds. That was for everything including the rings, licence, clothes, flowers, food and cake. My father had very little money saved up compared to my mother so she agreed to pay for the wedding out of her savings.

At the same time as she was planning her wedding with my father, she was also making plans to buy basic goods for her first home as a newly wed. She wrote down in her diary a plan of action and lists of all they would need so as to be able to look after my father in their first home.

My dad had taken an interview a week or two before

the wedding and got a job to go to after they were married. There was a house that went with the job, his first experience as a single-handed gamekeeper.

The owner of the estate and shoot, his employer, owned a chain of butchers' shops known as Grays of Worcester. The estate was called Hope End estate and it was situated at Wellington heath near to Ledbury.

They travelled by train after the wedding and moved in.

Their new home was a bungalow right at the side of the new boss's house. It was in a very nice, quiet spot next to a beautiful lake where Elizabeth Barret-Browning had sat and written her poems in the peaceful surroundings of a gazebo which looked like a turret on the edges of the lake.

The bungalow sat only a hundred yards away from the edge of the lake, a beautiful spot he recalls, with lilies on the pond in the summer and tiny green Grebes lived there all year round.

Dad said you can still drive right up to the lake to see it to this day.

My father said he heard that his boss had been born with his legs back to front but he never knew if it was true or not. He seemed to be quite able bodied to him.

Apparently he was a very nice man and was very good to my father knowing that it was his first job single handed and that it would be hard work.

As it was his first job working at his own speed and abilities, he still felt that he was learning, and over the first few months he asked other local keepers that he met in the course of his work for their advice and discussed any problem that came up within the job.

He said that he learnt a lot in that first year and his boss was very pleased with him. Dad said that he reared a thousand pheasants in that first year on his own and he would go and see one of the older keepers, Percy Cox at Eastnor and another on Lord Biddulphs' estate near Ledbury to get reassurance about what he was doing. He said that they were very good with him, giving out tips for rearing and generally supported him and each other when it was necessary throughout the year. He felt he could call on them at any time, and says now that he was grateful for their help and support. He knew they had a lot of knowledge of the countryside and a keeper's way of life and he wanted to model himself on these two men, hoping that one day he would be as knowledgeable as they.

It was in that first year that he got his call up papers telling him that he had to report for duty to serve two years with the army.

He took his papers to his boss, and explained that he could not go and leave his young chicks he had just reared. It would be a difficult time to leave them as they were so vulnerable, some only a few days old and dad was still right in the middle of the rearing season.

It turned out that the new estate secretary had filled in the official papers describing dads' work as gamekeeper and not farm worker or vermin destroyer as he had up until now been described. Apparently if your work was on the land it was considered important enough for you to stay there and continue with it.

Between them they managed to defer his call up until the following year.

By this time my mother was expecting their first baby and my older brother, Gary George White became the first child of the family, born in August of 1952.

Within a few months dad had to leave his work behind when his second lot of call-up papers finally arrived in May.

His boss asked that after he finish his time of duty that he come back to carry on with the job on the estate. Dad agreed at the time and went off to report to Shrewsbury to do his training, as was expected.

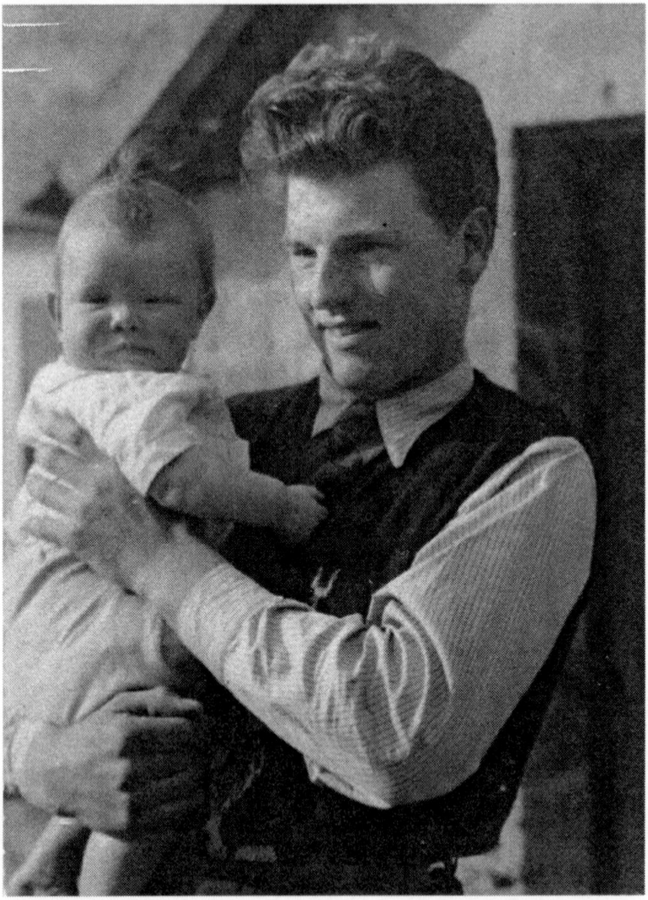

ARMY YEARS

Whilst he was in the army his former boss sent him ten a shillings a week so that he would come back to the job, but dad decided as time went along that he would look out elsewhere for work when he came out so as to gain more experience. He said that he felt a bit guilty about taking his former boss's money but he did tell him eventually that he wouldn't be coming back to work on his estate and the money stopped arriving.

Meanwhile mum had a dilemma as she would not have a home to live in while dad was away in the army. The bungalow went along with the job and she couldn't stay there for two years and wait.

She decided to call her family, be brave and go home if they would allow it. She had her newborn baby to think of and could not think of what else to do.

She went back home to Wray in Lancashire and was welcomed home again by the family.

Within a short while she found work again. She had willing and readymade babysitters in her brother and sister, whilst she went back to the looms doing the twilight shift once again at the silk mills in Bentham.

In her diaries she wrote down once again her details of work done in the factory and it showed that she still received seven or eight pounds a week even if she only got to work on three or four looms doing the twilight shift. It was very well paid work as there was skill needed to be able to run a number of looms at once. She had to be able to load and fix each loom if it got stuck or needed attention but she had learnt over the years to do this quite efficiently. After all she had done this job since she was fourteen, learning from scratch.

She saved all the money she could whilst once again helping out the family financially, awaiting my fathers return from the armed forces.

During this time dad had completed his basic training at Shrewsbury. He was generally a few years older than most of those that had been called up as he had been working on the land, being exempt until the paperwork mix up. He said he hated being there, but had to do it as it was compulsory.

During training they were taken on long runs in Wales over the mountains where they all became very fit. Dad said that he thought that he was very fit before he started the training but improved on it even more.

The instructors would take them to one side of a mountain and point out to the mountain opposite, telling them all that they had to run down one side of the valley and go up the next one to where they were standing. He said it always looked a long way across the valley. Sometimes the opposite mountain would be almost unseen because of the mist that covered it but there would always be marshals and instructors along the way to let you know where you were meant to run towards.

Dad was used to running marathons as he had done it since his early teens. It wasn't a problem to him. If you got there first the instructor told them they would get a bar of chocolate and a thirty six or forty eight hour pass for a weekend leave. He said that he had to try his best to get the pass and many times he did.

The trainees were taken from Shrewsbury by a small train directly across to the west and into Wales for a days running marathon. They would be instructed in the daylight going across the valleys and when it got dark they were put through their paces again, but this time in the pitch black. The men were told to head towards a light in the distance which was the finish line

He told me that as he was used to walking about at the dead of night doing his job looking for poachers so this was not a problem to him. He found his way quite well running along the routes he and the others had taken previously on the daylight training. He had taken note, getting his bearings as to where he was and his general surroundings. He knew where the river crossings would be shallower and where to cut across to bring him back along the route to join the others and go on towards the finish line. He told me he didn't want to get a soaking in the river he would have to cross as it was so cold. When he did miss his turning on one occasion and went along with the other trainees he came across a couple of the instructors who would dunk the men if they didn't want to cross. They had to in order to get to the finish line. On this occasion he challenged them and told them if they wanted him to get wet then they were coming in with him as well. The instructors backed off and let him pass. He walked through in shallow water, only soaking his feet up to the knees. They both knew he was in the boxing team and he meant what he said as they had seen him in action in the ring of a night time.

He had a lot to fit into those few hours when he did get the pass to go home, going back home to see the family and getting as much shooting in as possible. He got to go home a few times during his training because of his determination to win and be first across the line. It helped he was so fit and was grateful he had kept on running throughout his teens.

It was whilst he was out on one of the long runs over the Welsh mountains that he tripped up as he was going over a bit of rough ground. He told me he put out his hands to save himself as he fell and clasped a piece of golden rock that was amongst the other rocks and pebbles as he had fallen. He believes it was a nugget of gold. He said it was huge and it filled the palm of his hand. He carried it back from his run to the barracks but there weren't many hiding places in the army camps to hide it well and someone stole it from his hiding place, not long after he had hidden it.

It was after he left the army he found out the area near Dolgellau, where he had been taken to on his runs in Wales, was well known for its gold mines. He always promised himself that he would go back and investigate further, which he did with us children in the family, taking us all to the mountains' surface where he had run across during his army years. He found that far below was a deep mine which produced gold. We walked down the pathway towards the river where people were seen to be panning for gold dust. When asked if they found some they showed us small amounts making my father very excited. It was gold found in these mines which was used to make our present Queen Elizabeth's wedding ring along with other jewellery and was also used for Royal coronets and crowns.

I went with him quite a way into the mine hearing the tap, tap of miners in the distance still trying to earn their living out of the mountains core. Along the walkways there were deep pools of water where once there had been tunnels. These pools had rough planks of wood and metal bars placed across them so you wouldn't fall into them. As he considered it unsafe for me to go any deeper into the tunnels dad sent me back to the mine entrance and the family so he could carry on and investigate further. We went to watch the people panning for gold along the river whilst we waited for him.

He told us when he came out that he had found a man chipping away at the sides of a wall and dad had insisted he give him a piece of what he had found that day as a memento. He showed us a small piece of shiny rock he had been given and he has kept it all these years. He had apparently told the miner what he had found all those years ago on his army training runs and the miner had put the piece into his hand as a kindly gesture.

Gold found in Wales is considered to be worth three times more than standard world gold these days, as it is so rare, not being found in huge veins as in some mines throughout the planet. One hundred percent pure gold has been found in small amounts, some of it nearer to the surface than in other areas. Many of the mines have now been abandoned as such small amounts were found. He considered the lump of rock which he found to be gold and the genuine article, not fools' gold as some have since suggested. Who knows? Only the thief who stole it could verify if it had been genuine. Dad had hoped to have it tested when he was on leave but never got the opportunity.

During his basic training he had been asked what interests he had before joining the army.

Obviously the army knew that if the men had an interest they could further, they may well enjoy their time better, and promote team spirit within their ranks.

Dads' hobbies of running, boxing and shooting fitted in well in army life although he said that he didn't want to be there at all, even though he knew that he had to go through with it. He decided that while he was there he would make the most of the time there and learn everything he could in order to better himself for the future. He knew that he would need other skills in keepering when he came out, and he particularly needed to know how to disarm a man and how to defend himself in armed and unarmed combat. This was for all the poachers he knew would have to be caught in the course of his daily life as a keeper and it was important enough for him to be able to handle himself and others in an acceptable way. He was already very fit and capable physically, doing all the training that was required. He also wanted to be able to learn the right way of filling in an incident form as he knew that it would be needed in his job when he came out. He was given all the instructions whilst he was there as details were very much a part of army life so he found, being methodical was an integral part of training.

He had joined the boxing team and went on long distant runs most days as part of his training having done so for most of his teens. By joining the team he found he was treated better and had much better quality food at his mealtimes, such as steaks. They looked after their boxers it seemed and fed them well, allowing them a better diet and selection.

Dad decided that he would like to become a P.T instructor and given the training to do just that as well. It was just the start of some intensive training in the first few months of the army.

At the start he was also interested in joining the military police and after he had qualified as an instructor, he undertook more training with the regimental police and passed all his exams.

Also as part of his training he undertook rifle shooting

as an extra activity to become one of their marksmen if he was called upon to do so. He was very good at it as he had done it all his life anyway and it was the only time he would be able to do any shooting practice with a gun. Whilst in the army he couldn't fire a gun unless they told him to. This was very limiting for him but he had to accept it. Very little instruction on handling of firearms was done in the training as far as he was concerned other than to assemble and disassemble them. To add a little more incentive he was paid five shillings more per week for the added activities that he had taken on and trained for. He was also given a marksman's badge to be worn on his arm that had two crossed rifles and laurel leaves on it.

Finally after all his training he was asked if he wanted to go to Kenya or Germany, and decided on Germany as it would be better since it was a home posting. This eventually resulted in his being sent to Osnabrook where he became part of a small team of six policemen on guard trying to keep the rabble of squaddies in order.

He helped look out for a thousand men who were let loose in the nearest towns of an evening. Dad was called out many times to arrest and collect mainly drunken soldiers, taking them back to the army barrack cells for the night after they had become boisterous after picking fights either amongst themselves or with the locals.

He had to discipline the men and often took them round the P.T courses as part of their punishment the next morning after they had been arrested. He said that he didn't like to shout at them but it was his job and where he could, he would be fair with them. He would sometimes make them do press-ups if they wanted a cigarette or promise them a run out in the fresh air if they had been cooped up for quite a while in the cells. If they had been particularly bad boys, and had to stay in the barrack cells longer, he would take them out on the assault courses to work off their pent up energy. He would make them put on their full kit, making them carry it all around the course. Most would be glad to be out in the fresh air after being cooped up and this was an incentive for them to behave themselves, even if it was only for half an hour or so. If the men had been very bad and had to serve more than twenty eight days they were taken away to a better, bigger facility a few miles away to do their time. There was a limit to how many cells there were at the barracks, only having six regimental police in charge of a thousand men. Apparently they were pushed for space sometimes having only six cells.

He remembers there was one name which stuck in his mind throughout the army years. This man was regularly brought back to the barrack cells as he was always in a spot of bother when he was allowed out into the town. His name was Corporal Richard Scratcher. My father smiles as he tells me this corporal was more commonly known to all of the men as Dick Scratcher.

He recalls an episode where he was out in the fields on an exercise and had made a temporary camp with some of the men. It was early morning and just getting light when he had taken himself off to the nearest riverside for a wash and shave. He preferred to do that than use the wash facilities that the army had provided out in the fields. He tried not to get too friendly with the other men as it was difficult not to treat them the same if he got to know them well. He found that it was easier to arrest someone if he didn't know too much about them and tried to distance himself from the main bunch of squaddies in his control.

He had slept out in the open, a small distance away from the others that previous night, as it was a warmer time of the year. He had found a bit of a rut on the side of a bank where it looked a little more comfortable in the deep thick grasses. He says if he had not moved and got up from where he had been sleeping only minutes before he wouldn't be here today as a huge tank went over where he had just lain, moving through on its way during early morning manoeuvres. The men in the tank would not have seen him down in the long thick grass. The tank went right over the spot he had lain only minutes beforehand and would have crushed him. It was a close call and he is so glad that he always wakes so early in the day naturally and on this occasion it saved his life.

On some days there was different work that he could do by being a dispatch rider, taking messages all over Germany by motorcycle. He would volunteer to do the long runs as he would, often as not, love the long drives through the forests and woodlands of rural countryside Germany. It didn't seem to matter he was away for most of the day as the army allowed him plenty of time to make the drops, so he would take his time and find some enjoyment whilst he could. He could casually look over the hedgerows and go into the woodlands and forests, stopping if he saw anything of interest. He saw lots of deer and black vicious looking wild Alsatians that would wander about wherever he went.

He would often make detours so he could get a glimpse of the local wildlife over there. He told me he had often been chased by packs of Alsatians in the forests. The German forests were very big and would cover many miles of land and the dogs would roam freely. He told me that the foresters who worked amongst the trees owned some of the dogs, who were allowed to wander around as they were so far from any towns or villages. Apparently the dogs would give chase just for the hell of it as he believed there was so little traffic around, it must have been something for the animals to do as a pack and to follow a moving target. On most occasions he would eventually lose them after a few miles travelling. It didn't seem to worry him at all as he was used to dogs, having been around them all of his life. He just remembered they seemed a little wilder than those he had been used to at home.

However there was an incident with the dogs he recalls on one of his earlier assignments when he had so many dogs giving chase he decided to hide up in the loft of a barn he come across on a previous assignment. The dogs had apparently chased him for miles and were fast, keeping up with him well. He left the bike quickly, climbing the step ladder up to the loft pulling the ladder up with him quickly. He was stranded there for many hours as they knew he was there and he told me they would have torn him to pieces if he had come down. Eventually they all slunk away and disappeared back into the forest one by one. He remembers he got back very late to the barracks on this occasion but no one said anything about it to him as it was just another normal dispatch riders day and he would always have to report back to the orders room on his return no matter what time it was as long as it was completed.

He missed the English countryside and being able to go shooting. He was not allowed to shoot in the army unless they gave him permission, which wasn't often enough he said. He missed doing what he loved to do at home in his job and on these occasions he went in search of the local wildlife, whilst looking out for different species as he drove through the forests. He looked for any similarities in the bird life in general and the surroundings.

HOMESICKNESS

He missed my mother, Joan as well as his baby son and at night would write letters to her whilst lying on his bunk. My mother said that she wrote back to him every day he was away. He was so homesick he tried to write his memories about the countryside at home, memories flooded into his mind of his childhood antics and such happy times as a teenager and also courting my mother up on the moors.

Here is an extract from those notes he wrote:

"Looking back on my life I have had a very happy time all along. I reckon it was the fact that I always loved the countryside, and I mean love it!

It brought me in contact with all kinds of wildlife of the English countryside.

Starting from as far back as I can remember, it would be when I began going to school at the age of five. My father used to take me to school on his bicycle. Every time my father used to leave me at school I would cry. I would cry my eyes out!

After a time I got pally with some of the other school boys. Together with my brothers we would go bird nesting with my cousins and of course it soon got known that we were all owners of very crude catapults. In later years it would earn me quite a lot of money.

By the age of eleven I had become a very good shot with the catapult. We would get together and see who could hit a bottle or tin that was thrown into the air. Without bragging, there weren't many that could hit it more times than me and my brothers. I remember one particular time after school hours three of us killed nineteen sparrows. Didn't we have fun!

The next thing we began to think of was guns! Some of the other boys had got them for Christmas.

I got to know of a boy who had just left school and had a Diana airgun. He wanted fifteen shillings for it. It had a very weak spring and would only shoot a pellet about fifteen yards.

But to begin with we needed to get the fifteen shillings.

My brothers and I saved every halfpenny we could get and to finish with we sold quite a number of birds' eggs which we normally saved. Normally we wouldn't have got rid of them for anything.

That's to say that our first gun was a bit different.

We eventually got the money together, as pleased as can be; we handed over the cash, all pennies and halfpennies.

Having got it we were like dogs with two tails!

There was more on the ground at that time and we used to go under some thick Yew trees that were close to our house. Quite a number of Blackbirds fell to the gun although half the time it wouldn't go straight or possibly it was us who couldn't shoot straight.

Time went on there weren't many birds that we didn't know. I would go to any lengths and spend hours in trying to find out more about wildlife.

As we lived quite near to the Broads I had every chance of taking a rowing boat. This I did more after leaving school as I had a bit of money to pay for it.

As far back as I can remember we have always kept ferrets and it was a regular thing to be out at least once a week with them together with a couple of fast Lurcher dogs where we picked up quite a number of rabbits.

One Sunday morning when my brothers and I were out rabbiting, we got fourteen. That was one of the best days that we had round that time. We were quite pleased that those Lurchers could pick up a rabbit inside of fifty yards. It takes a good dog to do that regular. A rabbit was worth two shillings each and we were as keen as mustard!

We also found that there was quite a lot of sport to be had in knocking a pheasant over.

One particular afternoon when we thought the keepers wouldn't be about on the next estate, three of us went in one of the woods which had quite a bit of cover in it where the rabbits and pheasants would squat. We knocked thirteen rabbits and five pheasants over with our catapults. From then on I couldn't resist having a pull at any rabbit or bird I had the chance of.

Round Salhouse district I was well known for my skill with the catapult. What I enjoyed immensely was to go in a corn field and stand at one end. I could hit those rabbits on the top of the head pretty well every time. The most I killed in one field was thirty one, all with the catapult.

The game keepers round that district didn't like me with the old bitch. I have walked around with her on a moonlight night along the side of the wood. She would put her nose to the ground and follow the scent of a rabbit. All of a sudden I could hear her lumbering along in the wood. She would strike and there was a squeal, next minute she was at my feet with a rabbit. Very rare she struck a rabbit more than twice, if that and they were all alive.

I might say that these dogs were bought when they were about six weeks old and trained by my father as soon as they could follow him. I have seen them catch at about four and a half months old, not regular but they have caught them. I often annoyed the keepers round there, we could walk where we wanted and have all the sport.

When I had to steal my fun how I enjoyed it.

As time went on I started work on a farm and it didn't appeal to me but there wasn't much work around there. I just lived for knocking off time so I could plan out my route for the night.

By the way, I had a very comfortable home and had no reason for chasing about the way I did.

Like most men I started courting and the girls got to know about my trade. Even out with these I would have a fourten pistol and a catapult in my pocket.

I had a keeper walk by eying me up and down suspiciously and after he had gone I went to go the other way home and knock a brace of birds down on the way.

After a while I realised there was just one life for me and that was to become a gamekeeper.

This I did by putting an advert into a well known keepers' magazine. I remember I had several replies and asked for an interview to a job in Lancashire as an under keeper.

There was a trout and a salmon stream. The salmon were in the River Lune. There were also grouse up on the moors, several hundred acres which belonged to the estate which was situated in the Lune Valley.

I was very keen and naturally pointed out at the same time that I knew nothing of keepering.

I thought to myself that I could tell a few tales about the other side of it though!

At last I had got the job that I wanted. I loved the guns

and all the fun was there for the sake of walking and creeping round after it.

I remember the first time walking through the woods as if it was yesterday. I thought I was better than the fox that runs across my path.

But first of all I ought to write a bit about my lodgings which had been fixed up for me by the head keeper on the estate. The village was situated in the bottom of the valley with a stream trickling and winding its way through the centre of the estate into the Lune Valley.

One rather important thing to me looking back was the first day on arriving there. After tea I went out for a stroll round the ground trying to find some of the boundaries and general lie of the land.

I noticed there were quite a number of Carrion crows and magpies about at which I had to try my hand at killing.

There were also a nice lot of rabbits about and I knew that I was going to enjoy doing the job.

On returning from this little walk I made my way through the village back to my lodgings. As it happened I couldn't find the house as it was in among several more and I wasn't sure of the one that I was looking for.

A young woman on the side of the road stared at me as if she knew I was lost. So I went across and asked her if she would direct me to my lodgings. I found out after, she had guessed who I was, as she had heard there was a new keeper coming to live here.

Little did I guess that this young woman would one day be my wife!

So to get back to the story, the head keeper gave me my orders as to what was to be killed in the way of vermin. He said carrion crows, foxes and magpies were the worst.

I really had a good time and thoroughly enjoyed getting up early in the mornings for then I found was the time when most vermin were caught unawares. They got less when there were more people about.

Walking quietly along the side in a wood I saw a hawk glide off among some trees. It had risen from the ground about forty yards away. I went to the spot and saw a wood pigeon which had been half eaten. Knowing that the Sparrow hawk would be back before long I put a trap to it, which I usually carried in my shoulder bag.

The next day I had him.

These hawks are a menace to the game and small birds as every keeper knows.

There was one particular spot along the tops of the wood right at a junction where I always kept a baited trap set. I remember taking eight cats out of this trap in a fortnight.

Several people asked me down the village if I had seen anything of their cats, but no I didn't.

I often would take a large old black ferret we had and tie him out about thirty yards away from a hide with him jumping about and an old crow lying a few yards away from him. It attracted all kinds of feathered vermin over the decoys. I have shot numerous carrion crows, jays, magpies and often whilst waiting there have been a weasel or stoat come along the hedgerow and I have had them as well.

I got the head keeper to get a .22. It was a Winchester repeater holding fifteen bullets and didn't I have some fun with that!

I got used to it and could often kill an old carrion crow sitting on the top most branch of a tree carving his head off at eighty yards. The furthest I ever killed anything with it was at one hundred and fourteen yards. It was a wood pigeon eating some hawthorn berries on top of a high hedge.

At the time I slipped a long .22 bullet in as these carried a lot further. I found the short bullets were not very accurate after fifty yards in that rifle.

There were a lot of stone walls round there, they would go right up over the moors and there is nothing I would like better than to take my dinner and spend a whole day up there, particularly in the woods that were skirting the moors itself.

I remember going along one day when I saw a stoat stick his head out of the wall about ten yards ahead of me and he made a noise like two stones being knocked together. He drew his head in then and the next time he put it out he got a bullet through his throat and out of the back of his head.

Continuing my walk along from that little incident I saw something moving out about seventy yards from the wall. It looked like a rabbit and yet I wasn't sure so I made my way out to it very cautiously. When I got twenty yards from it I could see quite plainly it was a dead rabbit lying on its side but at the same time something was moving inside of it.

All of a sudden, a large dog stoat backed out of the rabbit skin he had been feeding from. I think at that moment he either saw me or smelt me and went tearing off back to the wall.

I didn't fire as it would have been a hundred to one shot against hitting him. I had a better idea.

I got the right way for the wind and came up behind where I had seen him vanish. I put my hand to my mouth and gave a little squeal on the back of it. After doing that a couple of times I saw him coming towards me. He jumped into the wall; stopped for a few seconds then jumped down again and came on.

When I fired he was about twelve yards away. I got him

through the shoulder. It was the bitch stoat that I had got only twenty minutes before. It looked as though I had made a clean sweep of those two.

Yes I had some wonderful times up on the moors especially when it was a shooting day and didn't I look forward to the twelfth of August.

My employer didn't shoot a great deal himself and more often as not the head keeper sent me with two or three other chaps off the estate. We never used to get big bags, usually fifteen to twenty birds on several occasions when standing in a butt.

I have seen a large pack of grouse coming straight towards me. I have aimed at a bird and there has been two drop.

My brother Hado came up on the moors with us sometimes as he was also as keen as mustard, and a very snappy shot he was too.

I remember lunchtime in particular when we had all sat down and were enjoying the scenery. I looked across at my brother and I could see that he had finished his lunch too. We decided to have a scout around just handy as the others were not quite ready.

Well, we started off and had gone about a hundred yards when my Labrador which was working about twenty yards ahead of us put up a lone bird. It only got about twelve yards before it was down. There was a big cloud of feathers floating away from where it had been. I looked at my brother as if to say "I made a good job of that!" I found him staring at me as if to say the same thing.

I pulled my empty cartridge out and he did the same thing. We shall never know who actually felled the bird.

After the dog had retrieved the bird we carried on a bit further. All of a sudden two grouse got up straight in front of us. I downed the one nearest to me and swung on to where the other one would have been but it was on its way down too. My little brother could hit them every bit as good as me.

One day we went up on the moor with some friends of my employer. They were policemen. We only killed sixteen birds but what a good day it was. The number of cartridges we fired between us was anybodies guess.

They were using twelve bores and my brother a sixteen bore and I a twenty bore. It rained very hard all day but it didn't stop us in any way at all.

We had a wonderful day up there and on the way down there was a large pack of grouse that got up on the flank for some reason or other. Just one of the birds came back all along the line. The two policemen emptied their barrels at it. When it got to my brother I thought that was it, but for some reason or other it didn't get touched and it still came on towards me. It was up about forty five yards; I gave it a long lead and pulled the choke.

I saw it stumble and then it fell and I was very pleased. It was my best shot of the day.

Going home at night I would tell the girl (who is now my wife) about all the different little incidents of the day.

The way she would listen got me, she was patience itself.

When I started rabbiting and had to get round my snares and traps at night she would come along with me.

I was in my element taking the rabbits out and setting up again. One night when I had quite a lot of rabbits in the snares she was with me as usual. She called out to me and pointed to a pile of rabbits that I had laid down and she said that one of them appeared to be trying to get away. I didn't take much notice at the time but when she called me again I saw for myself and got up to go from where I had been resetting a wire, to run after it. I had only got a few yards when down I went head long and head first.

I had put my boot straight through another wire. It ended up with a good laugh!"

My father kept himself as busy as best he could in the army throughout the normal day so as not to get upset just laying there wishing he was home again. He said a lot of the men in their free time just lay on their bunks and got depressed because they had too much time to think. Dad had the running and training to do as well as his part in the boxing team which now on reflection was a good thing and made time roll by faster as he was so busy. He made sure he didn't get a lot of time to himself.

Here is another short extract of words he wrote in that free time when on his bunk, of childhood memories in Salhouse:

"One dark and windy night, a friend and I went into a large apple orchard in Norfolk. I won't mention where it is. In two and a half hours I knocked thirty two pheasants off those apple trees. There were quite a number hit besides that, but we were satisfied. As I pulled back the elastic my friend was underneath with the sack. He grabbed the bird by the neck as it fell and put it in the sack. That was definitely our best night out!

I lost a lot of sleep since, remembering walking round those orchards, but it paid me well and I wouldn't have missed all that fun for all the world.

Up until now I had never seen a badger but the head

keeper told me where there was an earth in an old quarry. He also said that he had trapped a badger some time before where it used to slide under the bottom rail of a gate. Anyway, off I go to find the earth after peering about in the bracken. I found a worn path which went for quite a way and eventually led me to the earth. I wondered what the next move would be having got this far. I made up my mind I was going to kill that badger. But that was easier said than done.

We hear so many tales about people trying to get them and some are not very successful.

After weighing it all up I decided on trying to trap him.

The first night the traps weren't touched and every night after they were sprung and occasionally had some long grey hairs in them and on telling the head keeper about it he said to pull the traps up and go and wait about fifteen yards from the sett at dusk.

This I did for several nights still very intent on getting Brock, but there again it was to no avail. I didn't see a sign of him at all. I tried trapping him on the runs at the entrance to the earth and as far down into the earth as I could reach and still no good.

We eventually got a man who had a terrier to come and have a go at it. This the dog did, very successfully barking for all he was worth yapping at him for ages

We dug for about half an hour and came down right on top of the badger. It had its back to us and he was scratching away for all he was worth.

The terriers' owner advised me to shoot it then as we might not get a better chance.

This I did and was happy. At last I had killed a badger.

Looking back that was the beginning of many.

One day I found a crack in the bottom of an old quarry where there were signs of badgers, and the usual scratching where they dug up roots, and the tell tale claw marks, where they went into their sett on the rocks.

I got some wire and made a large snare and pulled a sapling down and fastened it so the slightest tug would throw it back into the air, this of course was done on the edge of the run leading away from the sett.

After leaving it set for a week or so, it wasn't touched and I had been there every morning at day break. All the time I had been thinking of another idea. This was to put a trap at the bottom of the ledge where I could see they had been jumping down. This was successful. When I got there the next morning as soon as I came in sight of the spot I knew I had him, as all the earth had been dug up and the roots of the tree to which he had been fastened had been bitten and all the bark torn off as far up as he could reach. Yes, it was a nice boar. I quickly put a bullet in my .22 and shot him in the head.

That incident with the badger brings to mind another episode in the same spot just a few months later. One Sunday evening my young lady and I were sitting on a flat rock in the same quarry when all of a sudden from only ten yards away a fox came into view and raced away up the sloping bank as quickly and as quietly as only a fox can.

We got up to investigate immediately and found it had been using the same earth as had been occupied by my badger.

I remember on our way back that evening the old vixen, as she turned out to be, gave one or two of her blood curdling screams that echoed through the valley. Naturally I was there the next morning with my traps but on entering the quarry I saw two little cubs moving about outside of the earth. I could have easily killed them both with one barrel but as they were very unsteady on their feet I decided I would try and catch one of them. I laid down the traps and gun and bag racing forward. I had about twenty yards to go to get to the set. They made it, though as they got to the entrance, my hand came in on them. I touched the one but the force of my dive had made me scrape all the back of my hand on the rock.

There was only one thing to do now and that was to wait at dusk for the vixen to return to them. This I did. I didn't see a sign of her but she knew I was there though. All her yells went on for some time. I must admit somehow I didn't feel so brave sitting there waiting for her. Every time she screamed my hair rose on the back of my neck.

I didn't get her that night but I trapped the cubs and she walked into it four days later."

During his time in Germany he didn't manage to get any leave home at all as he had done during his training, before being posted. He didn't want to be away from home or his wife and child.

However whilst doing his training, when he had won all those marathons across the mountains in Wales to get his thirty six or forty eight hour pass home, he went home to Wray in Lancaster to see my mother. Unfortunately he decided that shooting rabbits was far more interesting as he hadn't been able to shoot for months. Now he regrets he didn't spend more time with my mother as he says that he was selfish only wanting to go out shooting.

He said not only had he to shoot the pigeons and rabbits but he would have to sell them on as quickly as he could by taking them to Mac-fisheries in Lancaster by bus and train, in the bags and suitcases he had begged and borrowed to do the job whilst on his leave. This would have to be done before he left to go back to the barracks and knew it would take a bit of time and effort on his part and sometimes had to be done in the very early morning before his own departure back to Shrewsbury.

He wonders to this day how the drivers of the busses would allow him on with all the blood dripping from the bags and feathers all over the floor of the busses, piled high with as many as he could carry. He says the other passengers would carry on as normal without a backwards glance. They might have thought something but they never said a word.

He often enlisted the help of others including his father in law with getting the stuff to their destination. It was one mad rush to get all the birds on and off the busses and trains as quickly as they could.

He recalls in those days you could still send a dead rabbit unwrapped but tied up head to foot, with a label attached, to anywhere you liked in the country. He did it when he thought that his Mother needed a rabbit for dinner, as he didn't always know if his brothers were getting them for her to cook as often as he had done when at home. He always remembered his mother and kept in touch with her by letter when he could even when he was in the army.

He recalls on one of the letters she signed off saying "I must close now as I have a bee in my back passage!" The mind boggles.

In an incident whilst out on a scheme near Osnabruck when all the men got upset stomachs having drunk water from a trough they came across close to the camp they had made. They had made camp in a sandy area full of pine trees. There were apparently a lot of places similar to this around Germany. The men had to dig into the sand with a spade and erect a canopy over the camp, lining it with another sheet for the ground. The cooks were the only ones to have proper tents.

A trench had to be dug for the toilet facilities. This had to be done very quickly as the matter was becoming very urgent since the men were going about with their trousers round their ankles most of the time. There weren't enough facilities for all those men. Most men had been thirsty on arrival at the site, as had my father.

Two posts had hurriedly been put into the ground to one side of the camp for the toilet facilities. Another post had been laid across between the two for the men to sit on. A trench had hurriedly been dug along the back of it as it was an emergency. The trench and posts were extended over the next few hours due to the number of men wanting to go at the same time.

All the men would sit in a row baring their backsides with as many as were able to fit on to the post at a time.

Someone took on bets as to how many times they each visited the facilities in the eight hour period. They put in a few coins, keeping a tally and getting ticked off on each visit.

My father won the pot with twenty four visits.

THE GYPSY CARAVAN

It was in his second year in the army that he was brought home from Germany on compassionate leave. Mum was pregnant with their second baby and had high blood pressure finding that she was having trouble coping with her difficult living conditions as well as looking after her son. She had written to the army to ask if my father could come home to help look after his son as she was ill and heavily pregnant. She told me she had also enlisted the help of one of the authorities of the time to assist her in getting him posted locally back to England. Young Gary had broken his leg after a fall and life became difficult for her on her own.

She succeeded and dad was brought back to Cowley barracks, Oxford, and had to serve the remainder of his time in the army there. He didn't mind, he was very pleased to be back in England and closer to his family. He was allowed to live outside of the barracks as long as he reported for duty at six thirty every morning until his time was up with the army.

The base had married quarters of course but he wouldn't allow mum to come and stay there with him, as he said he wouldn't keep his wife and child in a place like that.

He would go around of an evening after his work was done and ask people who lived local to the barracks, if they knew of any houses to rent for his family to live in. However it was my mother who found a job as a live-in housekeeper for a while, so as to have somewhere close by. It was for an elderly lady who had a large house close to Cowley. Along with the job came a room for her and Gary. This was only a temporary arrangement until they could find somewhere to be together as a family. She told me the lady that she worked for was very kind to her in the time she stayed there.

Whilst she was up in Lancashire mum had worked the twilight shifts and bought a few small things in readiness for when dad got out of the army, like some linen and china.

She had of course given most of her wages to her Mother once again for their keep, but first had taken small amounts to save for herself and her new family. She had managed to save a few pounds again and when at last they found an advert for a caravan for sale, she was able to pay for it. It was an authentic gypsy caravan, on a proper caravan site not far from the barracks. It wasn't very big but at least they could call it home.

It cost thirty pounds to buy and they would have to pay ground rent for the site, which was twelve and sixpence a week. Dad said if they still had this gypsy caravan today, it would be worth a small fortune in today's money.

It was a traditional painted wooden gypsy caravan on high wheels with little steps that led up into it from the rear. There were wooden double doors that opened out and the steps could be pulled up behind you as you got into it. It was decorated and painted in the traditional style on the outside, and on the inside it was panelled out with polished wooden walls which mum said were beautifully put together.

Inside there was a chest of drawers to one side and a bit of that would pull out to make a tabletop. At the back there was a double bed with some lockers over it. On the other side there was a small range fire that could be cooked on. It also came along with a single gas burner. Dad made up a small child's bed using a spring and some extra wood so it would lie flat when folded up in the daytime.

By this time they had acquired a small terrier dog they called Mac. He was from good working stock and my father had bought him for my mothers twenty first birthday. My mother had taken him back to her home village when she had nowhere else to go whilst dad was in the army, and Mac had been accepted into the family at home. Mum said they all loved him as he was so intelligent and such a character. Although he was mums dog he was a natural born and bred working dog who loved to be outdoors with my father. He would get up and willingly go off with him when he went shooting pigeons and rabbiting.

When mum had come back to live close to dad at the barracks, she brought Mac back with her and he slept underneath the caravan at night.

He would always be up and awake, willing to go along with my father when he came down the steps of the caravan to get a badger early in the morning. If my father laid a piece of string across his back he believed he was tied up and not get up or even try to move anything, except his eyes which dad said looked as though he was begging him to change his mind and allow him to come along with him.

When they had first got Mac as a puppy he went out for a walk with the couple and got really excited running down into a rabbit hole. He stayed there for ages barking at the rabbits deep down in the ground. He seemed to know exactly what would be required of him from that very early age. Dad said although he wouldn't come out for ages, he still allowed him to come with him whenever he put out his snares. However, one day he got caught up in a snare when he was about ten weeks old as he went ahead of dad. He did the same thing about a month later but learnt from the experience. From that time on he would mark every snare that dad put out and he would leap like a stag over every one of them. He never got caught like it again.

On the side of the caravan they erected a small tent like structure, made of tarpaulin that was used for their bath time, and to store anything larger they would need for the family. They had to make up a shelter for their own toilet facilities, an Elson bucket toilet, and they got a small tin bath too. Heating the water in those quantities was a bit of a problem as they only had the one gas ring. Mum said she would usually have a cold wash because it took so long to heat the water. All water on the site came from one tap and had to be collected by hand after a short walk to the centre of the site along a pathway.

Cooking was done on the slow burner of the built in range which had a tiny oven. If you needed anything in a hurry the gas ring had to be used. She would use a huge kettle and pots when it was bath time and it would take hours to have even a lukewarm bath.

Mum told me that as they lived in such a rural setting and were surrounded by fields of vegetables, they ate very healthily.

My father had permission by this stage to go onto the land to shoot the enormous amount of pigeons that harassed the farmers and their new seedlings. He was told to take whatever vegetables and fruit he might be able to use at home when he was shooting on the land. He had been asked to shoot the tiny birds, mainly Bullfinches that ate the cherries and plums and other fruits the small holders grew for their living. They came along in huge numbers at that time and were a serious pest to the fruit growers. He told me it was such a shame as he didn't want to shoot these birds as they didn't seem as bad as the pigeons. He hoped he probably frightened away most of them as he stood and shot the pigeons that flew in over the crops. In these fields they also grew cauliflowers, cabbages, carrots and potatoes. There were also rows of green houses which contained more delicate salad crops and which offered some protection from the birds.

My mother told me it was the healthiest diet she had ever been on in her life.

On this caravan park there was a family who lived in a double decker bus. They were called the Goodeys. The children of the family thought they were better than everyone else, as they could go upstairs to bed at night unlike others who lived in one storey caravans on the sight. There was also a single decker bus and only one modern proper caravan on this sight.

If you went on up further along the track which went through the site there was a family who lived in a tin shack. If they wanted another room for their family they would extend it further by putting up more tin and posts and sacking. You could apparently see this had happened a number of times as the sides of the shack had been added onto while they lived there. This family were working as rag and bone men using their horses and carts to go round the local villages and bringing it all back. They were very kind to mum when she came to live on the same site and they told her if she saw anything she may need on their carts as they passed her by to shout out, and they would stop. She told them she was looking to buy a silver cross pram for the baby she was expecting and they promised to keep a look out for one for her.

On this site there was only the one other real caravan besides theirs and this one could certainly be called different.

During his time in the barracks dad found that there were certain benefits he could put to good use whilst he served his time. He was allowed to stay with mum at night on the caravan site but had to report back to the army barracks at six thirty every morning for duty. He could hear reveille being played on the bugles as he was approaching the gates nearly every morning.

He used this time to get in his shooting and would often put out snares on his way to the barracks removing those he had caught overnight. If he were lucky he would kill a badger and skin it in readiness for sending to Horace Friend in Wisbech, Cambridge. He would be able to get a few shillings for it. He would save up his skins and feathers if he had got any worth saving and send them off parcelled up. There were also stoat, weasel and mole skins, jay, owl, and magpie wings, and magpie and pheasant tail feathers. All added up, he would make an extra few shillings or maybe a pound every few weeks. Some were classed as better or *"firsts"* as Horace Friend wrote back putting on his credit note that had been sent to him.

He had permission from all the local farmers having explained to them that previous to army life he had been a keeper and would be returning to keepering as soon as he had done his time. They were then quite happy for him to go and shoot and trap as they knew what he was doing. He could shoot as many of the pigeons as he could get in order to protect their crops as they came through. It was at weekends he would often have more time to shoot the pigeons and have to take them to the barracks to pluck and dress for the Monday morning.

	Telegrams: MOLE, WISBECH 19 JU 1952 Telephone: WISBECH 947/948				
Credit by **HORACE FRIEND**, Ltd.				
(DIRECTORS: HORACE FRIEND, JACK FRIEND)				
WISBECH, CAMBS.				
To Mr. G White					
	Rate each	£	s.	d.
FIRST MOLESKINS				
SECOND "				
THIRD "				
TAINTED AND EXTRA SMALL "				
RABBIT SKINS				
FOX SKINS				
BADGER OTTER				
5 STOATS—Firsts	2/-		10	0
1 STOATS—Seconds small			1	6
2 "	1/-		2	0
WEASELS—Firsts				
WEASELS—Seconds				
HORSE HAIR				
WINGS & FEATHERS				
1 b. Jay w'gs 6½			3	6
6. " 3			1	6
2. Large Owl				8
1 small				2
3 Centres 1ths 2				6
			19	10

	Telegrams: MOLE, WISBECH Telephone: WISBECH 947/948				
Credit by **HORACE FRIEND**, Ltd.				
(DIRECTORS: HORACE FRIEND, JACK FRIEND)				
WISBECH, CAMBS. 22581				
To Mr. G White					
	Rate each	£	s.	d.
FIRST MOLESKINS				
SECOND "				
THIRD "				
TAINTED AND EXTRA SMALL "				
RABBIT SKINS				
FOX SKINS				
1 BADGER OTTER		1	4	0
STOATS—Firsts				
STOATS—Seconds				
WEASELS—Firsts				
WEASELS—Seconds				
HORSE HAIR				
WINGS & FEATHERS				
		1	4	0

Of course he had to obtain a gun licence by this time. He was granted one from Cowley so he was then official so to speak to own and shoot a gun wherever he had permission of the landowners.

> **THIS LICENCE EXPIRES ON THE 31st JULY.**
>
> **GUN LICENCE (10s.)**   QR 006033
>
> GEORGE WHITE
> PROSPECT FARM.
> HORSPATH. OXFORD.
>
> is hereby authorised to CARRY AND USE A GUN in Great Britain and Northern Ireland from the date hereof until and including the *Thirty-first day of July* next following; the sum of TEN SHILLINGS having been paid for this Licence.
>
> Granted at Cowley Works at 3 hours 15 minutes P.m. o'clock this Eleventh day of August 1955
> by [signature]
>
> NOTICE.—1. This Licence will not authorise any person to purchase, have in his possession, use, or carry any firearms (as defined in the Firearms Act, 1937) in respect of which it is necessary to hold a firearm Certificate granted under the said Act unless he holds such Certificate.
> 2. Any permanent change of address should be notified to the County or County Borough Council in whose area the Licensee's former address is situate.
>
> *Insert full Christian Names and Surname IN BLOCK LETTERS.
> †Insert full postal address.

On these Monday mornings he would be so loaded up with pigeons tied together draped about his person as well as the bike that he rode to the barracks, you would hardly be able to see him as he passed you by. It made him happy to be able to have the freedom to shoot again and to be able to make a little more money on the side for his family.

He would take young Gary along, to give mum a break, still with his leg in plaster when he went out to get pigeons. If it was cold and Gary complained he was cold, he would place the warm newly dead pigeons around him to keep him cosy as he looked on at his dad shooting. The second baby was due soon and it would be another mouth to feed. In fact it was November of 1955 when Gail Margaret was born, the second child of the family. She was taken back home from the hospital to live and join the family in the gypsy caravan on the site. It was a little cramped but at least they were all together. Mum had got her pram in readiness from the rag and bone family on the same site they all lived and she stored it in the tarpaulin shed when not in use along with the tin bath.

When dad arrived for duty at the barracks, he would get the buglers to help him pluck the hundred or so pigeons in readiness to sell on. They would put the feathers in the bins outside the guard room and if it was a windy day there would be storms of feathers, often blowing right across the drill yard, and over the training men, but he says, he was never questioned as to these happenings. He said he regularly did this in his time on duty and got as many men onto it as he could so as to get it done quickly; usually it was the buglers who helped him out as they shared the same guard rooms as he. They would often be next door to the cells and the prisoners if they were bored and needed something to do, were encouraged to do some plucking to ease the boredom.

He had a thing going on with some of the other men as he was in a position of trust, and if you scratched his back then he would scratch yours. He would let you off if you were late, if you did something in return for him in the day. He said it worked quite well.

The cookhouse was supplied with some fresh meat on many occasions and in return he was given small rations of coffee, butter, sugar and sometimes cocoa. He would often find a parcel of goodies ready to take home with him at the end of his shift in the guardroom. The ready plucked pigeons would be all bagged up ready to be sent to their destination as well.

The men on the base would often buy the pigeons and rabbits he killed as they enjoyed eating them too. It was a change from the usual stuff served up in the mess hall and those that were allowed out at night would take them away with them to their families.

He also said the people who worked at Cowley works locally would always be asking if they could buy a good ex-army overcoat and boots, if any of the men could get them at the right price. Dad said that quietly the men at the barracks had a good thing going on in the black market.

He recalls a gypsy by the name of Pithers who would whistle as he came past the buildings of the barracks with a horse and cart. He would stop to allow his horse to have a pee on the side of the road along the grass verges beneath the windows. He would sit there whistling away when out of the window above him, would often as not drop into his cart a piece or two of the officers silver from the mess. Apparently the gypsy knew who to settle up with when he had sold it on the next time he visited and small amounts of cash would change hands. It would seem that the odd few bits went missing occasionally by a small number of men, even though it wasn't supposed to happen. He said he doesn't think that anyone else seemed to notice the disappearances as nothing was ever discussed and the officers didn't seem to notice any difference and no one was ever confronted about missing items. He said he knew it went on but could not ever confirm who had done it. Clothes would also go missing from a pile of part worn clothes that had been put in a corner of the stores. These were usually overcoats and boots that had been discarded after use and not needed very often. They were supposed to go back to the store rooms up in the tower room at the barracks. From there they would be taken to the army surplus stores and sold on. Some never quite made it this far. There seemed to be very little control over the inventories over this kind of thing and dad said if he was asked to get something then he would occasionally supply it if it was hanging around, just as a few of the others would do also. He says he knows *"it is perhaps not the best thing to admit, but it happened and there it is!"*

Dad said that he didn't want to be there in the army and it was against his will as he didn't ask to go in when he did. He had a perfectly good job waiting for him to go back to and he missed all his shooting and his new family. He thought that the army owed him something for keeping him there against his will as he was missing out on what he really wanted to do in his life. Out of these little extras he would have a bit more cash for food and rent for the family, so he didn't feel too bad about it at the time.

On questioning him closer about these matters he became a little vague as to whether this actually took place as described or whether he had made it all up. He did seem to twitch nervously in his seat and I rather thought that at this moment some authority was just about to arrest him. There was a slight sweat appearing on his forehead, and the twitching became more apparent. He made me feel nervous myself as he was looking over his shoulder constantly and speaking in low tones and whispers, making me doubt his previous tales slightly as to their authenticity.

Or was it his own father having deserted his post many years before whilst in the Grenadier Guards, who should have been guarding the Queen when in actual fact he was happily tucked up safely in the family home, a gamekeepers cottage in the woods in Norfolk. The guilt of knowing of his own fathers little secret had also finally caught up with dad as I watched on. He looked about ready to bolt out of the door!

I felt so nervous for him by this time that I had to break off note taking as this also started to affect my own bladder!

BONAFIDE VERMIN OFFICER

It was during this time just before he came out of the army he was approached by even more local farmers to help them get rid of the enormous amounts of pigeons that would fly in daily. They would see how many dad had shot out in the fields close to the barracks and how good he was at it. Pigeons were such a problem for the farmers especially in the spring as their crops were coming through and over the summer as the shoots became healthy. Pigeons were hungry and would eat a large amount of the crops in the fields.

One of the farmers suggested to him to approach the local Agricultural Committee about becoming a bonafide pigeon shot for the area. They readily agreed to this and he was allowed to buy cartridges at a hugely reduced price in order to assist him. These cartridges cost twenty four shillings per hundred.

The Agricultural Committee would supply him with a certain number of cartridges and the only way he could confirm or prove the numbers he shot was to send the birds' feet to them in large quantities in cereal boxes every week or two. He kept a diary of his kills for his own interest and the number of feet that he sent as proof. On one of his diary notes for March 1956 he wrote: "*shot 218 pigeons, also 9 Carrion crows, 8 Rooks and 19 Jackdaws.*" Another entry for the same week was: "*Received 250 cartridges, for 124 pigeons and 5 carrion crows.*"

In the end they trusted him in that he was actually killing the amount they had supplied the cartridges for, but he says he did it for quite some time. He would sell on the de-legged pigeons to the local butchers or whoever wanted to buy them, making two or even three pence each. He would even pluck them for Macfisheries in Oxford, who would collect the pigeons on a Monday morning every week he was there. He said they needed the money for the rent which had to be paid weekly without fail, and he had to get enough for mum to go and buy good food. He said he felt that mum should be eating well as she had not long given birth, and life was difficult enough with living in a small gypsy caravan with a baby and toddler and didn't need the extra burden of worry over money.

As his time was almost up in the army, he was asked if he wanted to stay on. He was told if he did, he would be made up from Lance Corporal to Sergeant but dad said he wouldn't want to stay any longer than he had to, he couldn't face a further four years doing this. He missed being on the land and being a gamekeeper too much. He was finally demobbed from the army barracks at Oxford and Buckinghamshire Light Infantry in May 1956. His trade or qualification as a civilian was stated as Vermin Controller on his papers, whilst his service trade was described as being a Regimental Policeman. He had served two full years. He told me there were two very useful things the army had taught him and reinforced whilst there; it was to get up early in the morning and be clean and tidy in yourself at all times.

Before leaving the army he had a bit of a mission in mind. There was a small bell tower on the edge of the barracks and it was usually used for storage of old clothes and such. In the tower there was a pulley system that you could haul the stuff up to the tower to put into the upper storage space there. Connecting it all up was a long thick rope. Dad liked the look of this piece of rope having eyed it up every time he had gone to the bell tower.

I asked him what happened. He assured me with a huge grin how he certainly wanted to own this piece of thick rope and fate must have somehow smiled upon him.

On the morning before his departure he was with two of the buglers in the tower, frequently called the keep, above the guard room. They had been assigned to get some of the stored gear out from the upper heights.

One of them had to sit in the wooden box, a bit like a dumb waiter, which was attached to the rope and needed to be hauled up on a pulley system so as to get up to the top storage area. The other one stayed on the ground and operated the rope. Dad was an observer on the upper level helping to load and unload the goods to and from the box. He watched in amazement at what happened next.

Suddenly there was shouting from the top of the tower as one of the men vanished from sight, there now being a hole where the lift should have been. The man and the box had disappeared rather fast along with a lot of screaming as he went down towards the ground below, making contact with a loud bang some twenty yards beneath. Dad looked over the railings and saw the squaddy from inside spew out onto the ground, rolling out from the box, landing flat on his back, looking up and shouting out every name under the sun. Because he was shouting and swearing so much it was assumed he was in fact okay and unharmed, just a little shocked. Amazingly the box was still intact and strong enough to withstand the impact with the hard ground.

Dad said he got his wish to have the rope which must have frayed and snapped through frequent use, but can't recall if he ever used it for anything now, having conveniently lost most of his memory once again of the events.

He did say though that the army must have owed him at least that piece of string and it could have been an extra personal payment to him for keeping him away from his wife and family, his shooting and his job.

Out of interest, in more recent years he met a man who told him that he was called in to dismantle this same tower in the Cowley barracks. Apparently after it had been dismantled, it was discovered that it was a grade "A" listed building and it should not have been taken down, but the deed was done. Too late!

He has a thing for string even to this day and many people who know dad, regularly see him using coloured bits of nylon, straw bailer, binder-twine, mostly coloured orange or blue these days, to tie up and fix just about anything that can be tied. It's in his pockets and his vehicles, carrying it wherever he goes. I have known dad to have tied up poachers over the years with the binder twine from baling which he had stuffed into his pockets.

ALL IN A DAYS WORK

Dad had been looking out for a job in the Oxford area well before he was due to be released from the army. He had served his two years compulsory service, and came out with a lot more knowledge and experience, which he found he would need in the future, more than with what he had gone in with. He had made good use of the army years and done his training as well as becoming much fitter to do the work once again as a gamekeeper.

He had found a job through one of his family in Norfolk. It was near to Ledbury in Worcestershire, not too far away from where he had been in the army barracks.

Along with the job there was a house, although it had a water supply it could not be used for drinking. There was no bathroom, but at least it was a roof over their heads. Drinking water had to be collected from the side of the road from a freshwater underground stream. There was water in the tap which could only be used for washing and it was dangerous to drink as it was full of lead and impurities.

My mother found it a very lonely spot with no near neighbours. She told me that my father would be gone for most of the day to do his work and she was left on her own for many hours at a time. She recalls hearing the tap dripping and said it was the only thing which gave her steady company throughout the vast time she spent alone in the cottage. When my father eventually repaired it by putting in a new washer she told me it was very quiet and she missed the steady noise it had previously made.

The house was within feet of the Chedworth Villa Roman site that had been discovered some few years beforehand, at Turpins Green on Lord Vestey's estate. It was a quiet spot deep in the countryside with no neighbours except for the roman site which backed onto the side of the wood at the side of the house.

Lord Vestey's family was known for its meats, as a butcher's family originally, and he and the family owned quite a lot of land around Oxford. This was a well-known shoot and dad knew of its good reputation.

He was one of six keepers this time and they reared their own pheasants under the broody hens in the tried and tested methods of old. Dad said he learnt a lot in his time on this estate.

He said there were many deer about on the estate and if they occasionally shot one they would pass on the better cuts to the boss or whoever had asked them for it. They would then feed the rest to the ferrets and to the many dogs they used for the shoot.

There were many foxes on this estate and all night you could hear the squeals of the rabbits as the foxes hunted them or when they got caught in the traps or snares.

At the keepers house they had a long drop toilet at the bottom of the garden and they had to use an oil lamp to go out to use it at night. Mum said that she did not like to go out after dark, as the squeals of the rabbits were so loud and very close by. When they got a better quality Tilley lamp, which shone a lot brighter, especially after having a low quality oil lamp, dad would take this round the fields as it got dark, to get the rabbits out of the traps and snares, leaving mum without any light until he returned. There were also rats running around her when she went outside, so she wouldn't go out in case they ran over her feet in the dark. She was sometimes pretty desperate when he got back and he would get an earful if she had been waiting a long time.

The house at Turpins Green was on a back road of the estate, reputably to be where Dick Turpin held up travellers as a highwayman many years before, so it was pretty remote.

The keepers' cottage where mum and dad had moved to was in the woods where the Roman remains had been previously discovered by a game keeper. The keeper had made his discovery some fifty years before whilst he was out netting rabbits around his home on the edge of the woodland. He found a section of Roman floor tiles whilst digging into the undergrowth, trying to dig a hole to put the posts for nets across an area of the woodland when after his rabbits.

Mac, he recalls brought home what looked to be a bone, he suspected, from the dig in the field at the side of the garden. On closer inspection it was found to be one of the artefacts from the dig. As they were so close to the Chedworth Roman Villa site he was always wandering off to have a run around and he would pick up the occasional interesting piece and bring it home. This was when mum became more interested in the Romans and their history as it was right on her doorstep.

The site which had been discovered had all been laid out for viewing as they had found it. For viewing in the fields, shelters had been placed to protect it from weathering. Obviously the site had been searched over the years and other pieces had been found scattered about in the fields and the general area.

Mum began to take more of an interest in what had been found on the estate in general. The whole field being so close to the house was on display for her to see whenever she wanted and she could discuss anything with the workers over the fence whenever they were out there. She had always been very keen on archaeology and history as she grew up and this took her interest more, to see it at first hand.

Lord Vestey was a keen fisherman as well as having a great love for shooting. He would on occasion bring along his grandson, to fish for trout in the river at the bottom of mum and dads' garden. Dad says this is the now present Lord Vestey and he must be in his sixties and wonders if he still remembers this time.

Apparently the estate is still known to be good today, holding on to its long-standing reputation as a quality shoot and dad said he was so happy to have worked there in his time. He got on well with all the other keepers and made new contacts with some of the older keepers, knowing he wanted to learn and know all that they already knew and become as wise and knowledgeable as they were, someday.

There was plenty of shooting and trapping on this estate. There were masses of rabbits and all six keepers would go out and net quite often.

They would run a long net probably at least three hundred yards long, along three sides of a field. They would put stakes in to secure the nets and leave one side of the field open to allow the rabbits to come into the field overnight. It would be about nine o'clock of an evening when they would run another net which was all ready to be unrolled on its pegs across the opened side, trapping all the rabbits to stop their escape.

The next morning there were so many rabbits trapped, that there were rabbit tails left sticking out of the holes where there were too many who had tried to get down inside. The keepers would catch what they could and pull their necks to kill them quickly, and use the ferrets to bolt them so they could shoot them as they came out of their burrows.

The rabbit numbers never seemed to go down and the keepers, dad said, would regularly get anything up to four hundred in one day. They would go rabbiting frequently and he remembers the biggest catch was over six hundred in one session.

At this time the under keepers would be expected to paunch the rabbits before bringing them all back to the head keepers house and putting them into the game larder at the end of the day. They all soon learnt that if you made a long incision from top to bottom, with their sharp pocket knives, you could throw the entire contents out into the long grass and undergrowth with a good flick without having to get your hands soiled at all. It made life a little better and they all got the job done a little faster and with less mess.

They would hang the rabbits on the fence in rows as they were done and then pick them up for the horse and cart to transport back.

Remember this was still the fifties and there was no other transport other than a bicycle, and the estate still employed men to look after the work horses.

During the rearing season some of the meat from the rabbits was cooked up and minced finely to feed to the young chicks. It was boiled up over fires in the fields or small huts on the rearing fields and mixed with other dried ground up meals and seeds.

This practice died out in the late fifties, early sixties, as new businesses realised they could do this themselves and supply the keepers with a dried protein rich crumb for the younger birds. It was also made into small pellets, to be fed to the birds as they grew bigger. Dad said it made his job a lot easier when this feed was introduced as it freed up time which had previously been used for the long preparation of the chick feeds out in the fields.

BEFORE THE JUDGE AND OFF WITH HIS THUMB

It was on this estate dad was taken to court over an incident with trapping, in the course of his daily work routine. He had placed a spring trap, mounted on a small platform at the top of an eight foot pole, to catch a hawk who had been taking his young chicks from the pens. This is called a pole trap. The pens were in the woods, just within site and very close by to the Roman remains open for public viewing. The hawk had regularly taken quite a number of young pheasants and the trap had been set for at least a couple of weeks before it was found by a passing visitor, a school teacher, to the site at Chedworth Roman Villa. He had seen the hawk caught on the pole in the gin trap and removed it to take it home to have treatment for its injuries but it had to be destroyed in the end. He then followed it up by making a complaint to the R.S.P.C.A who took the matter further, as new laws had just been introduced to protect these birds and the use of pole traps had not long been banned. In fact it was only a couple of months after the ban had been issued.

Dad was taken to court and ordered to pay a fine of two pounds with costs of three pounds and three shillings. When he was questioned by the judge whether he knew this was now an offence he apparently replied,

"Yes, I know, but I have a job to do and there it is!" He also told the judge the hawk had been having his pheasants.

It was during the November of 1956 that I was born and taken back to the cottage in the woods with my brother and sister.

Also, during the week I was born, my father shot off the end of his thumb in an accident. The cartridges were at fault and one of them backfired in the gun injuring him. Apparently the barrel burst with the impact. In hospital he had to undergo skin grafts in order to make the repair more permanent as the blow had taken off the top and nail of his thumb completely. My mother was in hospital giving birth to me as my father had taken Gary and Gail along with him to shoot when this happened. As my mother came out of hospital with me she came home to look after the family whilst dad went in to have grafts taken from his inner arm. When it didn't take he had another slice taken from his thigh. He hated to be in hospital and discharged himself, walking many miles home from the hospital in Gloucester. My mother told me he should not have put himself under the pressure of all this exercise as his skin was red raw against his trousers and bleeding well by the time he arrived home. Hospitals were an alien environment for him and he just wanted to be home.

The scars healed over the next few weeks but my dad was upset as he was unable to hold a gun to fire it.

The thumb is an integral part in holding and firing a gun and so he sued the company, Eley cartridges and was given some monetary compensation. This was not what he wanted as he missed being able to shoot. Money cannot replace that pleasure of shooting a gun whenever he wanted or needed to as part of his work on the estate. It would take many months before he could pick up a gun to shoot anything again with ease and he recorded in one of his diaries dated May 23rd 1957 that he had a nice shot, a right and left, the first since his accident the previous year.

He may have regained enough healing to fire a gun but in the years to follow he would always have trouble in gripping anything in his hand as the damage was permanent and he has dropped many a mug of coffee over the years.

Once again dad became a little more ambitious and ready to move on to pastures new so decided to look elsewhere for a keeper's job that would suit him. There was nothing wrong with the job he was in, but he had decided in his youth to move around so as to gain knowledge from different areas about the wildlife. Once he had learnt enough of a particular area he would want to move along. He knew by being in a slightly different part of the countryside it would bring new challenges and what he thirsted for was knowledge in a new territory. More recently we have discussed his ambition to move on to new territories throughout his lifetime, and he told me that it must also have been the genetics passed on to him from his gypsy grandmother, the wandering spirit, which has kept him on the move around the countryside all his life.

He placed an advert in the Gamekeeper and Countryside magazine to find his next job. He was hoping to once again find a singlehanded post.

The head keeper on the Great Westwood Estate at Watford spotted the advert and wrote to my father asking him if he would be interested in coming to that estate as an under keeper as there was a position available. He wrote there was a modernised two bedroom cottage to go with the job if he was interested in applying. Dad went for an interview and was accepted as one of five under keepers for the Earl of Dudley. We moved very shortly afterwards to The Greatwood Cottages, Micklefield Green near Sarrat.

THE MOVE TO HERTFORDSHIRE

The great Westwood estate covered five thousand acres of land which stretched from Watford in the south up to Kings Langley in the north. It stretched from Chipperfield in the west to Chorley Wood in the east. There were fifteen large woods and it had many areas that were planted up with game crops such as kale and swedes.

There was also a further thousand acres of land with shooting rights on the outer edges of the estate, and many smallholdings with more game crops that would ensure the game would stay put and close to home. It was a huge area to try and contain the birds, to keep them fed and watered in the right spot.

The house provided with the job at Micklefield Green, was on the edges of the estate where he would have to travel to get to work each morning.

The house had no electric, the bathroom was a tin bath and it had an outside toilet. But it was adequate. Mum always had to make the best of what she had in sometimes, quite primitive conditions in which they found in the tied cottages. All water was cold unless heated over the fires up until now, but this one had a copper which had a fire grate beneath it to heat the water. Coal and wood were given as part of the wages for the job to heat the house and the water. There was nearly always a plentiful supply of wood though if you wanted more you could saw it up in the woods, especially after the storms. If you were lucky many of the estates had a woodsman or forester who looked out for the estate workers keeping them supplied over the winters.

They had a forester at Great Westwood called Jim Prior.

Dad said when he had a chat with him whilst out and about in the woods one day working, where he was challenged to a game of darts down at the local public house. Dad said he went along there and had a few games with him. Jim was apparently a very good player and kept dad on his toes and they made a bet of a gallon of beer for the winner. Dad doesn't drink beer but he gained a few mates who did, as he always gave it away if he ever won. He would turn up at the pub randomly for a game or two if he had a bit of time to spare of an evening after he had finished his main work, already having seen Jim out and about in the woods that day.

Dad loved a bit of a giggle and would try to catch Jim out as he was well known for walking along in the woods with his nose deep into a newspaper. It was a regular thing with him, walking and reading. Dad said he didn't know how he did this and keep on the pathways so he considered he must have looked up occasionally to see where he was going around the twists and turns. He would follow the pathways along in the woods at the end of his working day to get home.

One day dad killed a fox. He propped it up on one of these bends in the pathway with a stick, propping its mouth open to show its bared teeth and looking as though it was still very much alive, and about to pounce.

Dad knew Jim would be walking along this bit of the pathway later in the early evening. He then lay in wait just far enough away to see if he ever looked up as he walked along. On this occasion he did and got the shock of his life on seeing the fox. Dad said it was a good laugh at the time and remembers the startled look on his face when he spotted it.

It turned out Jim Prior eventually told him that he was the News of the World darts champion, so was a good opponent with a very good aim.

Jim also had an electricity supply to his home and bragged to dad about having a television set. He had heard about televisions but never watched one before so it had to be done and they were invited round to watch it on occasions as the man lay on his three seater settee falling asleep. Dad said he must have passed wind in a continuous stream as he lay there, scratching himself, lazily, oblivious to them both. He rarely spoke to them in the time they sat there watching the novelty of his television. They tried to ignore his bad odours in their keenness to watch this new talking box, which far outweighed any negatives. Dad said *"Jim Prior may have been a very good darts player but he also had a very bad wind problem!"*

It was quite a few years later he heard Jim prior had been drowned in a lake in the Lake District. He believes it had been an accident whilst out fishing in a small rowing boat in one of the lakes.

All the cottages on the estate had open fires and some had Rayburn cookers which would take coal as well as the wood. These had good ovens and solid tops to cook on. Unfortunately this cottage didn't have one of these yet and mum had to use the fire for a kettle and small pots.

When it came to white goods in the kitchen, these weren't really available unless you had a supply of electricity. In those days cooking was done with burners and ovens from gas bottles if you didn't have anything else in the house.

It was at this house mum saw some advertising for a paraffin refrigerator. When she enquired at the local supplier in Watford, they ordered it in for her especially. It took a bit of time before they could get one but they did eventually and she bought it saying it ran very well for many years. For the first time in her life she could cool meats and milk and even make ice-cream for the family in the tiny freezer compartment. It was a technological breakthrough as she says they never had electricity up to this point and always had to use oil lamps and candles for lighting.

By this time dad was becoming more and more successful is his shooting competitions. He would go off on a Saturday usually, along with a few friends to locally organised clay shoots. This is when he realised he liked to shoot the sporting clays that simulated the natural game out in the fields, such as bolting rabbits, teal, high pheasants and such. He told me that although he could hit the clays at *"skeet"* shoots and *"down the line"* that he found them not interesting enough or challenging to him as a sport. He told me that if you stood there at the stands long enough it would be quite easy to assess the position of the clay coming out of the trap and make a kill every time as these clays remained in the same position throughout the shoot. Whenever he could he would go to shoot the *"sporting clays"* mainly. Often he would win one of the top prizes of a few pounds but sometimes the prizes would be such items as electric kettles and toasters or any small interesting kitchen equipment. However it was no good dad winning all those electrical prizes since we had no electricity. He always ended up giving them away or swapping the electrical item for cash or for something more useful. Later on when he thought there might be a possibility of getting electric supplied to the house mum made him keep a few items just in case. She put them aside to live in hope.

It was now the start of 1958.

The keepers' job was the usual stuff; dad was given his own beat, his own territory to look after on this huge estate and given his own responsibilities, being responsible for partridges and pheasants.

GAMEKEEPER AT WORK

I am going to give a description of the job as a keeper for those who would like to know more and what it entails, within my own fathers life history. Although there is more to the actual day to day work than is described, a keeper needs his wits about him tuning into what is in his environment as he works in the countryside. Whatever is about on a day has to be dealt with, whether it is vermin causing trouble, poachers or just basic physical work that needs to be done. Tuning in becomes a natural talent most keepers adapt to over the years. Some keepers are born with it whilst in others it continues to grow, and the senses heighten. Dad told me he knows every bird which twitters in his environment and whether it is a mating call or in trouble or making warnings calls to the rest of the flock. He fully understands their ways. He has become at one with his environment in the real English countryside.

The keepers year went along the traditional route of catching up in the late winter and early spring, of all the hen birds from last years stock for egg laying, then the hatching and rearing out in the fields during the summer months.

He recalls in that winter there had been a fair amount of snowfall, which had made it easier to catch up the birds as they were hungry and came out readily looking for food. Often he would catch up a handful at a time and they soon amounted when they were put into the rearing pens which contained them.

He would catch them up by putting in short tunnels of wire into the sides of the pens in the woods. He would throw in a handful of corn on to the ground just inside of the fence and the birds would walk in to eat it and be caught. They rarely found their way back out but as there was food provided they didn't seem to bother much about escape. The shoot would need about four hundred hens by the end of February to lay enough eggs for the season. Each of the keepers would take the hens they had caught up to the main egg laying pen. By the first week of March there would be fourteen cock birds, to each hundred hens, as well, and placed into the pens. If there were too many cocks they would only fight amongst themselves and get upset. Any spare cocks would be penned up in case they were needed and if there were too many they were sold on to other keepers for their breeding season, if their was a shortage on their estate that year. It was good to cross breed with pheasants from other estates as it made their stock stronger.

The hens still had to be fed and watered daily, and the vermin who tried to pick them off had to be dealt with too.

It is the keepers' main aim to protect his birds, twenty four hours a day and seven days a week, three hundred and sixty five days a year.

If one hen bird was lost to a fox it would mean the keeper also missed out on the potential chicks in the future.

There were always quite a few cock birds wandering

around the estate after the winter shoots that would go in search of the females, pairing up and laying their eggs out in the woodlands and hedgerows on the estate, if they were not caught up. The cocks always wandered onto the roadsides and across the fields, in their search for a female, you will see them in the early spring looking their absolute best, immaculate in colourings, and having beautiful plumage as it is their mating time, spring and early summer.

After the winter, the keepers would of course have to check out all the pens to be used to hold the birds out in the woods for the summer. These would have to be rebuilt and tidied up in readiness for the year's new hatch. This was a job which would need to be done after the shooting season had finished on February 1st and Cock Day was over.

Cock day was the day all the estate workers and beaters who had helped out all the year would get their chance to shoot the pheasants. It was the last day of the shooting season for pheasants and is traditionally used to cull the cock birds that wandered the estate, hence the name. Not many are needed for the rearing, and the hens are usually caught up from this time onwards in readiness.

There is and always has been penalty for shooting a hen bird on cock day and since they are considered valuable for their egg laying qualities at this time of year, it has been the mistake of many a novice gun out for the first time on a rough shoot to have to pay a fine on finding it was a hen bird they had just fired at and shot. What is even worse was if you shot and killed an ornamental pheasant that was still about on the shoot. Heavier fines were always given for these rarer birds and are still today as they are really only for show and it's good to see them wandering about in the wild amongst the other more common pheasants.

When he wasn't fixing up his pens and stiles across the ditches and over into the fields, dad would be out pigeon shooting on the estate. There would always be so many pigeons flying in to look for the new shoots poking through the soil on the fields. They would eat the crops before they had a chance to grow through if left to their own devices. He would get a few pence for each one he shot but his boss Lord Dudley gave him an allowance for cartridges as well, but dad enjoyed shooting so much he always wanted more than he was allowed and it was the sale of the pigeons which paid for these.

It was about this time dad got even keener than he had been in clay shooting at local events and went off for an hour or two in the daytime at the weekends to take part in them. He would take along a couple of his friends and they would all as often as not take part in a practice round, and then compete, thus having a bit of a social life as his friends watched his growing expertise. It was from this time onwards he was making a name for himself as he would often get a prize in the top three or even took the first prize of the day. First prizes became more and more frequent. It was often a small amount of cash in those days, not enough to get excited about he tells me, but it would help out in paying his next entry fee and some of his cartridges. He would then go back to work, quite happily, and carry on doing whatever work was needed for that day. It was a short break in his working week which would pay off in the future years to come.

Most clay shoots are held in the spring and summer months and the main competitions would be held all over the country. It was not always possible to go to these as they would take up too much of his time away from work, since the pheasants still needed to be looked after. It was sometimes okay to go when the other keepers were working as they would cover for him. There never seems to be an official day off for a keeper as it is considered to be twenty four seven job, but there are times when he could have a little more time off for his shooting, such as the early spring when the pheasants are just laying, after being caught up. As long as the eggs get picked up from the pens a couple of times a day and they are left with food and water then he will leave them in the care of his babysitters, usually the wife and kids.

On the larger organised clay shoots, when he got really good at it, like The Game Fair and the annual gamekeepers shoots he would compete against a larger amount of competitors and other keepers like himself. On theses occasions it would be an all day event as they would have to shoot a hundred clays in all and then there would often be a shoot off for the top scorers of the day to establish the winners and runners up.

He would have to organise someone to look after his patch on the estate and cover the feeding and so forth until he returned. He would on his return go and look about to see if all was well. He had a duty to do and he was very committed to it he told me. He would also arrange the hatch around any large event in the summer so as not to be so busy, having to put the eggs under the hens so they would be still sitting, or after the chicks had hatched out. The other keepers would chip in and look after them as and when it was required. A lot of the time in these years shooting events started to be held over two days but he could not afford to take the time off to attend both days as his work would suffer and he had to do his best at the shooting on the one day he attended.

The springtime was also a time to get all the foxes, squirrels, stoats, rats and the rabbits as they were by this time all breeding themselves. Their numbers increased and would all be looking for food, namely the game and the eggs which would soon be laid on for them like a feast out in the fields and hedgerows.

There were always lots of vermin to control and it was in February and March when the keepers organised rough shoots asking their friends and farm workers for a walk about on the estate. On these occasions there were huge bags of pigeons and a few rabbits, hares and it was always hoped there would be a fox or two. They would also get a few jackdaws, jays, crows, magpies and squirrels if they could, and anything else that could be a threat to the young birds during the rearing season.

On some windy afternoons in the early spring, dad told me he would shoot anything between fifty and a hundred pigeons on his own if no one else was available to come along with him on the day. When he considered he had enough pigeons he would take them to the game dealers or local butchers to sell on to be eaten.

Friends would bring along their terriers to get the rats which would breed like mad. The men and dogs would have a few days at it and get hundreds. The rats would, if left to their own devices, quickly breed into large numbers, get into the corn bins and eat everything they could get hold of, if not culled like this. The dogs would all get a much needed outing doing what they were best at, after the long winter break. The little dogs were very keen and eager to go along as most of them had been trained since tiny puppies for this type of work.

On this estate there were also badgers which did a lot of damage in the woods as they dug underneath the edges of the pens, lifting up the posts and fencing, so allowing the young birds to escape in their panic. The noise of them snuffling and squeaking about also disturbed the young chicks. A badger will attack and kill the chicks to eat if they can't find anything else, and the young poults are in captivity, enclosed by wire, so are easy targets for them. When the young poults are only just learning to go up to roost in the trees and shrubbery at night, when they are first released from the confines of the pens, they cannot escape so easily out of harms way.

Right up until the sixties it was not illegal to kill the badgers, as they were considered to be a nuisance and just vermin.

Dad would arrange for some of his acquaintances to come along with their dogs for the days' shooting and they would flush out the badgers if there were too many of them on the estate and causing a nuisance. The badgers would build such large sets and rubbish from it would be scattered about all over the place, sometimes knocking over posts and fences, pulling up the bushes and undergrowth making it very noticeable in quiet woodland. The badgers would breed and take out their youngsters, if left to themselves, out into the woods to look for food. They would if allowed, take over the area and disrupt what the keepers tried to do in the release pens knocking over bins and water butts and digging anywhere they fancied.

The men would sometimes use gas or smoke to get them out of the deep holes they lived in but nearly always they sent in the dogs to chase them out or worry them enough to make them move.

The men would use spades if necessary to dig down into the sets as sometimes the dogs would get so excited and needed to be dug out. The dogs would just bark and snarl at them unable to back up or turn if they met head on.

The badgers would be shot in the head as they poked out of the sets. It was always a clean kill. Not all of them were shot because there has to be a balance of all wildlife and dad said he wouldn't be without them even though they were so much of a nuisance. Everything has its place in the countryside. Today they are not allowed to be destroyed as they are a protected species although they are known to carry T.B. Only those people who are officially nominated by the government are allowed to cull the badgers, usually only on farm lands occupied by cattle, which are believed to catch T.B from them.

Dad remembers going along the track one night whilst in the land rover, seeing the badger a little too late in the headlights to totally avoid hitting it. He said he felt the bump as he hit it and having gone over it stopped the vehicle and got out to see where and how he had injured it. He walked around the back and found it was still very much alive and ready to waddle on where it had been heading to down along the drive as if nothing had happened. He said it looked totally fine and had absorbed the shock. He looked out and about for it to make sure it had not been injured in the next day or two but found nothing untoward. This he says just shows how hardy a badger is.

He also recalls hearing the squeals of young badgers down by the riverside in the early summer. On investigation, having crept up to the river bank without being seen, he says he watched as two youngsters swimming behind the mother, she getting out and up onto the bank using the tree roots as her anchor, was now making noises for the two to follow her. They had been trying to cross the river which was fairly high after rain had swelled it out and were having trouble trying to get out. They had to keep swimming back in the quite strong current towards the roots which over hung the banks and were making a bit of a fuss about it, squeaking and grunting, and calling to their mother for assistance. They tried a number of times but had to go further down river as they weren't as successful as their mother. Eventually they scrambled out, each finding a way to climb up in the undergrowth on the sides of the river bank, taking a few minutes each to do it. They were being resourceful and determined and eventually successful, carrying on behind their mother, in a convoy off into the woods towards their destination.

I was only about two years old when my father took me and my sister Gail down to the woods to see something very special.

He told us we both had to be very quiet as we were taken up onto a high bank after a trek through a wood. We were told to lie down in the thick bracken on our bellies and just wait to see what happened as we looked over the ledge below us. We were well hidden in the thick undergrowth and remained silent throughout. We didn't have to wait long as the badger family walked towards us back towards their set entrance, the two youngsters squealing and grunting as they played along the pathway.

They chased each other about in front of us in an entertaining manner, as we both looked on enthralled by them. This is one of my earliest happiest memories as it was the first time I had seen a badger family out in the woods and at so close a view point. It was a moment I will always remember.

FOXES AND HENS

A fox is such a clever animal and my father has over the years killed many hundreds if not thousands of them. He has missed quite a few in the earlier years but developed a love hate relationship with them and he has great respect for their intelligence. He has had to lay in wait on many a dark night in order to catch them out, either as they come out to hunt, or in the early morning when they are on their way back to their young with their kill for them to eat.

He recalls an episode where he had set a trap, a snare, and he went to check this early one morning. Having found the post that should have had the snare attached to it now missing; he followed a trail going out and across into the wheat field. As it had been pulled across the crop, which was now ripening, he saw a bundle in the flattened corn and the post sticking out from beneath it. It was motionless.

He walked around the bundle very carefully and quietly to see if anything was still attached and wondered if it was a fox as it was strong enough to pull out the post, and drag it. If it had pulled it this far it may well be dead by now.

Amongst the ripening corn he saw a tiny patch of golden hair, a slight shade darker than the corn and then stood there to see if he could work out which way the fur was lying so as to know which end was which, as it was obviously a fox which was lying low and feigning death or injury.

He didn't have his gun on him as he was just following the trail of flattened corn, having left it in the vehicle, since he was only checking his snares and didn't think he would need it.

A bit of quick thinking was needed and he made a slow grab for a fence post close by. As he went to thwack the end he thought was the head, out popped the fox, already having worked himself free from the snare with no obvious damage, running at full pelt across the field and to freedom. All dad could do was stand and watch in astonishment at how the fox had freed itself from the snare and had then made a run for it right in front of him. Having no gun on him to shoot it was a rare thing in itself as he and his rifle would normally go everywhere together.

It was a very lucky fox who got away that morning, the snare didn't get him, neither did the fence post, or even a bullet. He lived to see another day.

The only thing about a fox that has been very close to being had is that it will learn not to trust a certain situation again and they become even more wary and harder to catch out. They will lift up their nose and smell and listen very carefully after a near miss, even the slightest rustle in the bushes will get them edgy and they will be off as fast as they can. It is the town fox who has no worries about getting food as it is often put out especially for them when they live in towns and villages as people seem to think they are cute.

These foxes sometimes find themselves out in the

countryside one night having gone on a wander probably looking for a mate.

These foxes lose their inhibitions and often come too close to danger and before they know it have lost their lives to a bullet in the head. They are unafraid of humans so will get up close to houses and people, which for them is unfortunate when they get onto the private shooting estates.

It was still the fifties and it has to be noted game keepers were well known to be a law unto themselves and they could kill just about anything they deemed necessary, if it interfered with their job. They did this with traps, poisons and gasses, whatever worked best. They would have anything that moved if it caused harm to their young charges. It was the last time a keeper could do all sorts that are these days considered mainly illegal. It was in the fifties and early sixties that laws were introduced and phased in to protect certain forms of wildlife which the keeper has to adhere to. They would be fined if found to be breaking the law the same as anyone else.

It was the earlier years which gave keepers a bad name which the general public still refer to today, but now the roles have changed and the breeds which are in decline are now looked out for and protected by the gamekeepers and estate workers. In these modern times, they are often the only ones who get to see the rare birds out in the countryside and can report back to agencies to let them know of the existence of the bird, animal or even plants that have become rare. Game keepers are the custodians of local wildlife in this new era and have become more protective of the environment and all its creatures, since so many species are declining. Even the wild plants are under threat as new roads and housing estates are being built.

My father will spot an unusual flower like a sow thistle or rarer shrub on the sides of the road whilst out and about on his travels around the estate in the spring, and mark its position to keep an eye on it. If the local council mowers are due to cut the grass verges he will sometimes remove the plant to a new position in order to keep it safe. Even the tractor drivers from the farms will go straight over rarer flowers as they don't always seem to have eyes for these special plants. These days they are more concerned on how much ploughing or other work they have to get done on the day, as they seem to be under more pressure than they used to be.

As the keeper's year progressed the laying pens around the estate had to be ready and fox proof by the time the hens had been caught up by the end of February. In the fifties and sixties the pens in the woods would be surrounded by low electric fences fed by car batteries to help protect the young birds. These would have to be checked that they were working in readiness for when young chicks would be released. They would hopefully stop the progress of a wandering dog or fox and make them turn away if they touched it, giving them a bit of a kick. It didn't always work but was a good deterrent. The batteries would have to be replaced regularly on a turn around as their charge ran out.

The first broody hens would have to be bought in from the local farms and small holdings around the estate. Many of the locals kept chickens in those days and would sell them for a few shillings to the keepers for sitting on the eggs. They were mostly Well Summers,

Light Sussex and Rhode Island Reds, as they were all good solid breeds and settled down well to sit, being a good surrogate mother for the baby pheasants when they hatched out. A collection was made and the hens put in boxes in readiness with pot eggs to test if they were ready to sit. If a hen kept getting up and wandering around they were not really considered to be broody. The real test when a hen was ready was to put your hand beneath them and feel the eggs beneath her. If she pressed down onto your hand, she was ready for the job and a clutch of eggs. She would be given a couple of pot eggs to get herself ready for sitting and if she stayed sitting for long periods of time, she would be used out on the broody fields.

Down in the woods all pathways and rides along the edges of the pens would have to be cut by hand with a scythe. All the pens had to be cleared and pegged down where it was necessary and tunnel traps set in appropriate places alongside the edges too. These would be placed in the natural runs the keeper can see, where smaller animals follow there own natural pathways, winding their way around the woodlands. Snares would always be around in the woods along the regular runs of the foxes and rabbits.

Normally rabbits will naturally dig and cause a lot of damage if there are quite a few of them around the pens, sometimes uplifting the wires and making holes under the fencing. It was only now the rabbit population was getting back in numbers after the myximatosis years which almost wiped them out.

In his diary of this year, dad reports he has seen a second young litter of rabbits on his patch this week and this pleased him.

Apparently there were pockets of the rabbit population in various parts of the country which had not been affected by the myxamatosis, but there were not many.

Also in his diary for March he records he has heard the first Snipe drumming this year, saying it was a beautiful moonlit night at 7.50pm. He was out with his gun, a .22 and shot two pigeons in the moonlight as well.

Two days later he saw the first swallows, along with the first willow warbler of the year.

It was the beginning of April and he records he picked up the first pheasant eggs laid by the hens in the laying pens. By the end of April these eggs were put under the broody hens for the first hatch of the season

In mid April he heard the first cuckoo whilst he was out taking young Gary with him to shoot pigeons. Gary was allowed to shoot on this day and killed his first dog fox with a .22 rifle. It had been caught in a snare and was still alive, having to be dealt with quickly. All the snares had to be checked on daily and be reset if needed. When there were a lot of snares it meant extra time to get round them all.

Dad told me he regularly shot with a 28 bore gun at the vermin like the pigeons and foxes. He would take his gun whenever he went out into the woods so it was always on hand in case he saw anything. In the woods he and the other keepers would build new pens for the young poults ready to be released in the early summer. If they saw a rook, crow or jackdaw they would have it before they had any chance of getting to the eggs or youngsters in the pens.

Up until the mid fifties dad would have erected pole traps close to the pens. These were tall poles with a small platform which had a set gin trap attached to the top of it. Owls and other larger birds would come in to land on the tops, having first caught their prey from the pens and finding somewhere to sit and devour their lunch. Not a nice way to be killed or captured but it was legal in those days.

AQUAINTANCE WITH POACHERS

In dads' lists from his diary he says the pheasant eggs are hatching out at a good rate and there are plenty of blacks.

It is now mid May and it's never too early for the poachers to come out to see what they can get from the land. He would chase off young boys who came out of the nearest villages and towns. As the weather improved they wandered onto the estate in search of adventures. They would often be out with their catapults trying to get a rabbit or two. Not so many of them had airguns in theses days; catapults were cheap and easy to make and it was usually something for the youngsters to do in their free time and at weekends. These young boys would wander on to the private estates without really thinking too much about it.

It was on one of these occasions my father spotted a small group of young boys, probably around aged twelve to fourteen, walking along the edges of woodland on the estate. They each had a catapult and he watched them as he tried to cut them off by creeping round the woods ahead of them in the direction they travelled. They suddenly saw him and shouted out the alarm to run, scattering in all directions like hares. Amongst these young teenagers was Peter Jones who was only thirteen at the time and managed to escape by hiding in the laurel bushes after a short fast run.

It was two years later when he was fifteen that Peter was seen on the estate again by my dad, luckily not in the act of poaching and he spoke to him. A friendship which has lasted a lifetime was born.

Peter was a local boy living close-by to our home, on the estate it turned out, and he became a regular visitor when we moved to "Berry Bushes" when dad became head keeper. Peter was keen to learn all he could about keepering. He would help dad out on the rearing field in the summer and then amongst the woods. He came along on shoot days in the autumn and winter as a beater also.

I recall one of his daytime jobs when he had learned to drive was as a bread delivery rounds man. He would turn up of an afternoon and ask us children what cream cake we wanted to eat. He would throw open the back doors of his van and pull out huge wooden trays of mouth-watering looking cakes. To me as a four year old it was a wonderful sight and to be told I could have any one I liked was absolutely marvellous. He had actually done the bread round for the bakery and brought along the cakes that were going to be too stale to sell on for the next day. He knew my dad would feed them to the pheasants after we had picked out what we wanted. It didn't affect the taste to us though as this was a real treat for us. My brother Gary and sister Gail also tucked in with gusto and appreciation.

Peter would do this quite often, dropping the cakes round instead of taking them back to the bakery and the bins there.

I can also recall Peter hanging wallpaper in our living room as my father had no patience with it the previous week. My mother had asked Peter if he could hang wallpaper as she had frustratingly watched dad try to do it without any success and it was full of bubbles and lines. He had never done any decorating before in his life and had no patience with it at all, happily allowing someone with more flare for the job to do it.

Peter went on eventually to become a builder, buying a few acres of land locally and built his own property to live in, whilst helping the keepers out in his spare time, learning the art of keepering. He also started to hatch a few pheasants and partridges himself for his own shooting ground and he bred in the same way as dad, for his own land. He went on to acquire the neighbouring fields and farmland as part of a shoot which has grown over the years and is today very successful.

In his diary dad records he caught two youngsters on the estate who he says were full of excuses. This is only just the start of a very long queue of poachers who end up before the magistrates in Watford for the coming year. It would seem the locals in the towns loved to come out to the countryside for the evenings.

The hatch continues throughout May, keeping all the keepers busy tending the sitting hens out in the broody fields. This is a day and night job for all of them as the hens are so vulnerable. The hens had to be tethered to a stick as they were taken off the nests so they wouldn't wander off. Normally they sat on eighteen eggs in the nests at a time but smaller sitting bantams were unable to cover this many. The smaller bantams were used for the much smaller partridge eggs.

As soon as the chicks were hatched they were taken along to another part of the field along with the mother hen, to be placed in a larger coop so as to allow more room for the chicks to roam as they grew.

All the hens have to be fed and watered early every morning after being opened up to allow them some time to feed and to empty themselves. They usually happily settled back on the nest to sit for hours until the keeper comes round in the afternoon again. Out of eighteen eggs there were usually around fifteen pheasant chicks which would hatch out. The first few days the newly hatched chicks would stay underneath the hen to keep warm and didn't wander around too much. If it was a warmer day the young chicks would sit out in front of the hen in the sun and huddle back if there was any sign of danger or they got cold. They would push themselves under the hens' wings in the soft down of her feathers to keep warm and safe.

In this year there were up to four hundred hens on the field. Each of the coops was set at twenty yards apart, so they could be moved around regularly to a new fresh patch of grass. The corn and food had to be hauled around by hand as well. Carts were sometimes used with the horses but they had to be all loaded and unloaded as necessary. All the water had to be fetched from containers on the edges of the field. They would run a hose out to the nearest forty gallon drum which had to be filled. Dad would carry a bucket around with him always having to refill it as he went along the rows.

He would carry a small game bag made of thick sacking over his shoulder for the corn and meal. Bags like these were and are still carried by keepers even today, as they are useful. Each hen would be given a handful of feed as well as her water jar being topped up. This happened twice a day.

As the afternoon and evening went on and the light started to go, all the wooden fronts had to be replaced on the coops so as to keep the hens and chicks safe and dry for the night. The foxes could smell the hens and wait to pick off whatever they could get as they were an easy target if forgotten by the keeper. Lamps had to be placed at intervals around the field to help keep the foxes away and so if the keepers looked across they would be able to see if all was well.

Dad got some eggs from a golden pheasant and Guinea Fowl to put under the hens. He was interested in all the beautiful varieties of ornamental pheasants and birds. Mum was too and she asked my father to bring some to put into the small pens by the house as they were beautiful to look at and she would help keep an eye on them for him. At home he started to make collections of quails and unusual birds like the Lady Amerhurst pheasants in the aviary he had built especially, releasing into it a few more exotic birds as they hatched and grew. He had silky hens and small colourful bantams walking around the home garden and surrounding area. They would get up to roost at night in the woodland behind the house and occasionally they would be caught up and put in one of the pens, they nearly always managed to escape but would keep close to the house and garden.

Duck eggs were put under the hens as well as the pheasant eggs. They would be brought up in much the same way although there weren't as many of these. When old enough after being hatched, they were put on the ponds and fed in much the same way as the pheasants, being looked at twice a day, morning and night. There would also be some wild duck nests around to be kept an eye on. Wild partridges were also encouraged out in the fields naturally to breed as they didn't like to be disturbed as much as the pheasant chicks. They were better left to themselves naturally although some were still put under the broody hens so they could be guaranteed to have a few.

During the time the hens were sat in their coops on the fields it was a vulnerable time for them. They were at the mercy of tiny pests such as red mites as they were enclosed in a tiny setting. These mites could kill the hens if left to their own devices and had to be treated by sprays such as sulphur methadone and occasionally T.C.P. This was a bit of a laborious job as it sometimes had to be done a few times during the season to every hen that sat. The area had to be sprayed in the coop as well as the bird, and done as quickly and quietly as possible so as not to upset the hens too much.

All the keepers had to help out with the feeding and watering. The young chicks would mix with the others on the field but when the mothering hens called them back to her with her clucking noises, they would hurry back to their own coops. Each would know their own mothers call.

As they grew larger they would become more independent and it was just before they could fly that they were caught up to put into the sheds to contain them better. They would only fly about otherwise and attract the attention of passing vermin. If they were contained for a little while longer and allowed to grow on they could be transferred to the pens in the woods.

Dad remembers waiting to see the first flights of the youngsters about four weeks old as they realised they could fly. He said it was a wonderful sight to see on a warm sunny day, stretching their wings out in the sun, trying them out for size. He looked forward to this moment. It meant that they were growing up and it was another stage in their young lives which had been reached.

As more eggs were laid by the pheasants these were put under more broody hens. This was a very successful method as it was natural but very time consuming for the keepers.

Progress was in the offing as paraffin incubators had been on the market for a few short years. Keepers were starting to use them but they weren't really big enough for most estates to use very efficiently. The manufacturers were getting more ambitious and making them more economical and they were powered by electricity instead of paraffin. The big estates would over a few short years abandon this old system and install a series of huge incubators which were less likely to go wrong. They came along with a set of instructions which once used and taken in would become as automatic to the keeper as the once broody hen system of rearing, only quicker and more efficient. You didn't need to keep an eye on the hens and eggs overnight as they had always done out in the fields.

On this estate they were just starting to use the incubators a little more. The keepers would dry off the newly hatched chicks then put them out into heated sheds on the broody fields. They would be allowed out into wired off pens at the side of the sheds only going back at night by the heaters just as the broody hens would be doing with their chicks.

May was a busy month with all the hatching, feeding

and watering. The weather improved and the young pheasants flourished in the warmer weather of early summer.

It was around May when the farmers were out cutting the hay and grass along the sides of the roads and lanes when they often came across a nest of eggs. Occasionally they would have accidentally killed the sitting hen as she would be difficult to get off her nest, not wanting to leave it. The nests would not be able to be seen amongst the long grasses. The farmers would rescue the nest of eggs and leave them to keep warm in the sun. Sometimes they would leave a marker on the field like their jacket so as to mark the spot, until one of the keepers came past to collect them. They would do this often with the wild nests so dad would collect them and take them to put under a broody hen to finish the incubation time. As long as they had not got cold for too long they would be okay and would successfully hatch out.

It was also this month when as there were many young birds hatching out that the hawks would be out looking for their next meal. It would be a feast for them as they looked down along the hedgerows and fields.

The head keeper would be making arrangements for the farmer to help with the planting of his game crops all over the estate by May. It is vitally important to have a good relationship with the farmers on the estates where shooting is concerned as it can make or break a good shoot. The farmers in the sixties were starting to get into the high tech machinery and the newer ways of cultivation which included the new pesticides and weed killers on the fields, where beforehand there had been very little. A large number of estates let the main areas of land out for cultivation of arable crops and because of the more successful methods some farmers might get a little greedy and want to include the planting up of those parts of the fields that were given over previously to the game crops and the shooting.

On the Westwood Estate they were very lucky to have an understanding tenant farmer who went along with the way the keepers worked and understood the positioning of the crops, and why they were needed. They would all help out in the cultivation of the land and give assistance when it was time to plant up, usually late May and early June. Some of the seeds needed to be planted by hand so it was the right depth and thickness but once it was in, it needed very little care as they only planted hardy kales, swedes and greens along with the maize.

The wheat as food for the pheasants was grown on the estate by the farmers but if there was a shortfall of any of the grains in readiness for the autumn some will have been ordered ready to be stored at the farm and then taken out as it was needed and put out into the woods. Maize was bought in for the pheasants as well as being planted up along with kales and greens around the edges of the fields, more commonly known as game crops.

May went into June and the hatch would be intensified. There were hens still in the fields and the keepers' days were very long and hard. All keepers would be on call day and night in case of foxes and the vermin traps would have to be checked on regularly. Stoats and weasels occasionally sneaked up from beneath the nests and took whatever they could get and had to be watched out for. The men would often have to sit out in the fields and wait for foxes if they had left their scent around the field or been spotted that day. They would do this after closing up the coops as it was nearing dark, the lamps would be lit around the edges of the rearing field.

In dads' diary dated the 7th of June he writes he was making movable pens like mad. In that same week he also writes that he had two vixens and a dog fox snared on the edges of the release pens down the woods.

Some of the first young pheasants would have been caught up in readiness from around the fields to be released into the pens in the woods. They would be put into the movable pens and if the weather was considered good enough from late June onwards they would be taken to the release pens down on the estate. It was an ongoing thing as soon as there were enough of them to make it worthwhile to move on they would be transferred out. Many of the hens would still be amongst the poults at this stage as it gave the youngsters some security as she would continue to call them up and back to her if there was danger about.

Once again in his diary he writes for June 11th that overnight a fox had killed 18 of only 24 ducks around the pond.

Again on June 19th, he had taken one hundred and eighteen six week old poults to the wood, shot a carrion crow and trapped a weasel in one of his tunnel traps down by the pen.

The movable pens would have to be shifted around to a better position every week as the grasses became muddy and yellowed, to give the young pheasants a fresh base in which to walk around on.

He writes in his diary of finding ten dead chicks on the field and it may have had a few more. *"This fox will have to die!"* he writes.

The birds that were old enough were taken from the fields to the release pens in the woods by horse and cart, having been caught up and loaded into wooden crates especially for the job. The keepers would slip a board under the coops which contained the hen as well and lift it up onto the cart as a complete unit.

The crates had been stored down the farm in the barns and would have been brought out on the cart to the fields in readiness by the keepers a couple of week's before-hand. The coops were used only if the hen was going as well as the chicks.

All of the month of July, the young pheasants were carted off to the woodland pens, to be released. This was as they reached the right age. Most of the mothering hens were still doing there job of protection and many of them were taken along with the youngsters so they felt more at ease with their new conditions.

The crates were often loaded high to get on as many as possible in one trip. It would often be quite a way to the woods and the crates, although sometimes tied on, would bounce around and occasionally fall off as the cart hit the edges of a rut. They had to use the farm tracks and some of these were full of potholes and had deep ruts. The keepers would have to walk along beside the cart to keep the crates upright. If a crate fell off sometimes it was better to leave it where it was after putting it upright, so that the hen, if she was in it when it went over would call her young brood back to her when left alone.

The keepers would have to go back later when they had settled, in order to put a board or covering over the front of the coop or crate so they could be picked up and taken to the wood with the others.

The last hatches were taking place in July and the numbers on the fields were growing much smaller. They still had to be cared for as much as the others had been but the keepers would take it turn to do the work as they now had more young birds out on their own patches to look out for as well.

As soon as the pheasants were in the pens then the keepers' job was to take as much care of them as physically possible. They would still have to be fed and watered every morning and afternoon and as they were even more at risk from foxes and other vermin, the keeper had to become even more vigilant, even to the extent of going to check on them again as it got dark.

Many foxes would have hopefully been killed by this time, in the snares or with the rifle which was kept by the keepers' sides day and night. If there were very few breeding pairs around there would hopefully be less of a threat from them looking for food from his pens in the woods.

It was whilst he was out in the fields and on their way to the woods dad said they would often come across field mushrooms as from mid July. They would pick a few or mark the spot for the following morning to gather for breakfast the next day, when they would fill their hats or a bucket if there were enough of them.

If they went past snares they would automatically check on them as well and as they left the young birds, if there was an electric fence, they would check on the battery and whether it was sending out a pulse along the wire.

I remember when I was with him as he went along to feed sometimes, he would ask me to see if I would touch the electric wires and tell him how it felt to me. Maybe it was my age but I held onto it as though it was quite normal getting the kicks going up my arm. I must have been about three when I first did this. No harm done though. I remember quite enjoying the sensation then, but I wouldn't be so sure of it now.

It was during July of this year that my father discovered a nest of very rare white wrens in his beat. They were Albino and something of a peculiarity in the wood. My father was excited over them, keeping their location a secret as he didn't want them to be disturbed. He contacted someone who could perhaps take some film or photographs of them for him. He wrote to a Mr. J Hurlock of Nacton near Ipswich and invited him to come to the woods to see if this would be possible.

Mr. Hurlock wrote back saying he would very much like to try and get a picture using his telephoto lens as long as he had some good light on the subject matter on the day.

The gentleman duly arrived in the second week of August and was shown the site where they lived and had nested. Some twenty three feet of cine film was taken of the birds that day and a promise of a copy of the film and photograph was made. Unfortunately my father recalls that he never got this from him and never heard of him again. He said that he has never seen an Albino Wren since although they do crop up very rarely, just not on his patch again so far.

To get about quicker, dad got himself a motorbike so he could come and go as much as he felt he needed. He had ridden a motorcycle throughout his time in the army and up until this time had not owned a car. He would use it to get to the woods to feed in the early morning at first light and in the afternoon with his game bag full of corn over his shoulder. He would leave the bike as he got near and walk along to the pens.

As the weather improved the young pheasants blossomed and grew, trying out there wings even more so now they were able to fly and go up to roost at night.

It was during this summer that my father got to grips with his driving test. He wanted to own his own car and as he had a young family it would prove very useful.

It was about this time that my sister Gail had become unwell and it was found that she had picked up something from drinking water possibly from a well where we had lived previously. It affected her kidneys and she had become quite ill at times having to go for hospital checks regularly. My father needed to be able to take her to her appointments, so to be able to drive would be helpful.

He took a test in the early spring and failed miserably on a number of points. Having found his *"failure to pass statement"* of that time, I wonder why he may have kept it, as I would have been ashamed to have owned such a document as this. It included the improper use of gears and speed on approach to junctions and failing to take care in looking left and right before crossing a road junction or merging with one. As for a reverse into a limited opening with reasonable accuracy I can only use my imagination now at the very thought of it. As for making proper use of the handbrake and steering it would seem that he had plenty of room for improvement at the time. Having been in a car with him over the years I must say that his driving did improve dramatically, although my mother has said that he must stop looking along the hedgerows as he was driving along as she thought they would end up in the hedge itself. Of course he did just that on more than one occasion as she sat beside him. Driving straight into the ditch with the nose of the car sitting up in the hedge. Anyone reading this now will have realised when they have sat in his vehicles going along at speed, will be grateful for the fact that they are still in one piece. Wherever he goes my father will be looking anywhere but where the road is going. He tries to see who or what is about in the fields and luckily in the towns when he is driving he has very little opportunity to see anything other than the buildings around him, which is very fortunate for the people of the towns and villages where he now lives.

After plenty more practice on the private estate roads and with the help of his fellow keepers, my father passed his driving test and was allowed out on the open road by himself at last.

FREE AS A BIRD

The wire boundary fences were eventually lifted from the release pens as the birds began to fly over finally finding their wings. At this stage there were more birds on the out side of the pen than within its enclosure, the pheasants roaming freely around the wood and surrounding areas. They could often be found on the edges of the woodland amongst the now growing game crops, out in the sun taking advantage of the warmth and it was both food and cover for them to hide in. The young birds would be happy to stay if they had everything they needed right on hand, but if not would wander off in search of a better environment.

A pheasant isn't a very clever bird and all it can think about is food and water, fear and something else in the spring.

It was as soon as the birds had begun to wander away from their mothers on the broody fields that dad decided to use a whistle and call his birds at feeding time. It was his signal to the young birds that he was around and it was feeding time. He would carry this on as they were released into the woods, coming in off the edges of the field to eat the maize and wheat mix which he threw along the rides in the woods as he walked through of an early morning and once again in the afternoon. The pheasants would come in off the fields on hearing the whistle to feed on what he had thrown, knowing it was he who was calling them. After all they had heard this almost every day of their lives and this was quite normal to them.

A ride is a swathe or wide pathway which goes through the woods, having been cut with a sickle or mower by the keepers. This pathway would have been cleared in the early summer and kept low using hand tools on their frequent visits as and when it was needed if the grasses grew too long. It was where the keeper threw his feed and encouraged the young pheasant to come to when he whistled them up at feeding time.

The corn could easily be found on the ride by the birds as he threw it from his bag as he walked. He would check while he was there the wheat in the fifty gallon corn bins covered in tin was able to run free with extra food if the pheasants needed it. The young birds would run up to him as he walked about in the woods, getting to know him and trusting him, bringing their food.

The corn bins had to be kept topped up at all times once the birds were released and the flow of the free running corn from the hoppers checked upon each morning and night so the birds would be able to feed at will. What he threw about on the rides was only a small amount which would hopefully encourage the birds to stay near to the feeding bins in the wood.

He would have had to make sure there was always water in troughs low on the ground or in tin trays if there were none naturally in the woodland. Sometimes there would be a small pond or even a small stream which the birds could drink from but this was rarer. Usually a pipe network was set up leading off a cow trough in the fields close by or it was carted in on the back of a cart and horse in huge containers right to the pens. The containers would have to be filled by using a bucket from the trough in the field if there was one. This took time and had to be also checked on regularly. If the water supply ran out the pheasants would wander off to look for it so it is always important to have it there.

As the shooting season for partridges was the first of September, a whole month earlier than the pheasants, they had to be out on the edges of the woods in the game crops and headlands well before the pheasants. They had to be settled in, in readiness for the first shoot days.

On this estate they would be encouraged to breed naturally in the wild taking up their positions for nests wherever they felt comfortable in the thickets and long grasses on the edges of fields. They were regularly checked on by the keepers although they didn't like to be disturbed so this had to be done discretely and quietly.

Partridge eggs were collected from the wild nests if thought to be in a poor position on the estate and been hatched out under a broody bantam, in much the same way as the pheasants. It was the success of the partridge rearing on this estate when dad gave the other keepers some encouragement to collect some of the eggs they found. Hence because of the numerous nests that were saved out in the wild which made it a good all round shoot in the first year when he had started the job. He was keen to encourage the partridges to breed as the land had the right conditions for them and his boss was a particularly fine shot at theses small birds. He and the other keepers just had to make sure the fox numbers were kept as low as possible throughout the summer as they would have the hens off the nests as well as the eggs.

There were also stoats and weasels to be trapped but a lot of these were caught in the tunnel traps all around the pens. Dad said he could occasionally if stood very still when around the regular runs, have a stoat come running over his green Wellington boots. He had to be quick but he said he could stamp on them to make a very quick kill. There were more stoats and weasels around in the sixties than there are today, being seen more and doing a lot of damage to wild nests and in the pens during the breeding season.

Dads' friend's like Peter Jones collected wild partridge eggs from nests they came upon whilst out on the estate or in the course of their own days work and gave them to dad to put under a bantam hen to hatch. Over the season he got quite a number like this for the shoot as recorded in his diaries of that year dated June 22nd. He records also that he got ten French partridge chicks from ten eggs picked up from the wild the previous week.

As a young girl at Watford and since those times I have been along to the release pens out on the estate a number of times to help him to gather up all the dead young pheasants which had been killed by the foxes. There have been hundreds at times, as the fox is having some fun making a kill, one after the other. They will break the necks leaving them where they fall, going on to chase the next one. It becomes a game to them. They do it just for the sake of it, getting excited over the amount of birds that are in captivity. It is a depressing sight for any keeper which is why the foxes have to be culled as much as possible up until July when the birds are put out in the woods.

Once the young pheasants could fly they would go

up to roost as soon as it started to get dark. They will fly up and stay there till the first light in the higher trees and shrubs of the woodland so as to naturally protect themselves from predators.

Some of these predators were in the form of man and known as poachers and next to the foxes were the biggest threat they had.

IT'S A DANGEROUS LIFE

Poachers gave my father the biggest headaches and the biggest thrills of his life at the same time. He said it was a way of letting off steam, and as any fit man would like a bit of a rough and tumble if danger threatens his family, or in this case his pheasants.

Some poachers would often carry firearms, such as a gun or crossbow and were not scared to use them on the keeper if they were found down the woods on a dark windy night. They would often muffle a gun with old pieces of carpet so as to lessen the noise when it was fired, and thinking that somehow if they fired on the keeper it would not be found out or they would be able to get away.

Every eventuality would have been covered before they were approached by my dad to make his arrest. He would arrange with the other keepers if they could be called upon quickly to accompany him to the spot where the muffled bangs were coming from. They would surround the poachers on all sides if they could and be raring to go in to make the arrests. All the keepers seemed to like this part of their work and happily would creep up on the unsuspecting men.

The poachers would often use smaller guns like the four-ten as they could hit the birds out of the trees at close range as they were at roost. It was mostly when there was enough light from the moon to see what they were doing, and a wind to cover up the noise.

There were a large number of poachers from all backgrounds who were caught on this estate and had to appear at Watford Magistrates court to be sentenced. Often as not it was a small fine and the guns had already been confiscated from them on the night the incidents occurred. The keeper would in those days be able to make the arrests themselves, as they are to this day, as long as they are acting on behalf of the landowner and with his permission. Using a weapon just added to the amount they had to pay if they got caught as they had gone with the intention to use them to kill the birds.

In the fifties and sixties there were poorer families than there are today and poaching was a good way of making up the finances of a night time. They would not only take it home for the families but they would also sell on the surplus to hotels and game dealers and butchers who would in those days, give them a good price and no questions asked.

As the keepers were all concerned and committed to taking care of their beats on the estates very few pheasants were ever had in large numbers by the poachers. As clever and wily as they believe themselves to be they should never underestimate the skills of my father and the other keepers who always have an ear open to different noises and activities on their estate. As they get nearer to the scene of the crime taking place, there is often the smell on the breeze of a cigarette as the poachers will occasionally light up as they go about their search for game up in the trees. Cigarette smoke will travel quite some distance and my father will pick it up instantly in the air just as a fox will do so if there is a smoker around laying in wait for him.

Local residents and those connected with the shoot will also call on the keepers or nowadays make a telephone call to let them know of any unusual activities or noises which they are suspicious of.

This is a series of accounts as told to me, of what took place out on the estate, mostly during the autumn and winter nights, on hearing there were poachers around.

"It was moonlight and I heard muffled shots. I went to investigate who and what was about, heading in the general direction of the bangs. I headed across the fields silently and quickly, making sure I kept out of site, darting along the hedgerows and thickets of cover out of site to the poachers. It had been snowing in the afternoon and there was a light covering on the ground.

It was about one thirty in the morning and it was nothing unusual for me to be up and about at this time of the night. I was usually ready and waiting, wide awake listening out for trouble.

I had heard the shots in the distance and they kept on firing. It sounded as though they were muffling the barrels with old carpet. As it wore out, the bangs would be heard louder and it would have to be replaced and retied onto the barrel with string. I had come across this type of thing many times in the past over the years.

This gun sounded like a four-ten single barrelled shotgun and I had already counted nine shots so far. There could be two guns but they would both be four tens, but I wouldn't know until I got closer.

I walked along the thick hedgerows until I got closer to

the action which was just across the river from me. I had to creep up nearer so they wouldn't see me as I realised there was more than one of them with a gun. There was a small amount of moonlight filtering through the clouds and I could just make them out, both walking about beneath the trees. They were obviously picking off the pheasants as they went along, in the high trees of the woodland, shooting them off the branches as the birds were at roost.

Between us, the river wound around the side of the woodland and I had to get across it in order to catch them.

I crept silently ahead of them along the bank and waded into the river down wind of them, making my way across at what I thought was the lowest point. I would have to lay in wait quietly allowing them to walk up towards me. I couldn't let them see or hear me now I had got this far.

I knew the river like the back of my hand in the daylight but now I was just hoping I was along the right stretch which wasn't too deep as it was so dark to see. The moon had temporarily been covered by cloud.

I got up onto the other bank quietly, hardly having felt the coolness of the water across my thighs. I was lucky to have crossed at this spot as I also knew there were some very deep pools along this stretch of water.

I was right in front of them as they almost walked into me. They weren't expecting to meet anyone it was obvious, and they both turned immediately in opposite directions and ran in fright.

I was on top of one of them as he had turned, rushing towards the river, running to get away from me. He jumped right in over the high bank; I was right behind him, landing in the water a yard behind, only a split second later.

He had gone right under as this was one of those deep

pools of the river, and as he came up I grabbed his hair and pushing him back under again, holding him there for a few seconds.

I remember telling him he wasn't going anywhere.

Whenever he struggled and came up, I kept pushing him back underneath, until he could struggle no more and gave in.

I wanted him to be struggling for air. We were in six foot of freezing cold water and he badly wanted to get away from me. I just kept dunking him until he stopped struggling. He must have been scared I might allow him to drown but I wouldn't do that. He didn't know I wouldn't though! I was trying to control him, make him scared enough so I could secure him and get him out without either of us getting hurt any further.

I had my knee in his kidneys and I pushed him up into the roots of the overhanging trees alongside the steep sides of the riverbank. He was more concerned about staying alive at this point and allowed me to cuff his wrists behind him. I always carry a pair of handcuffs in my pocket for just such an occasion, as you do! He was very quiet and probably in shock at this point.

I said to him very quietly "call your mate." All the time I was in the water I was wondering where the other poacher had run off to. He still had his gun with him and I would have to get hold of him on my own as well as disarm him when I got this one out.

But my next thing was to stay as quiet as possible and get us both out of the water and up onto the banks a few feet above us.

It was to be a huge effort on my part as his hands were tied up behind his back. He was a dead weight and couldn't really help himself at all. So I used the root system to grab hold of and get a foothold in the deep icy water, pulling him up behind me slowly, laying him eventually face down in the snow covered grasses and undergrowth on the bank. I still managed to keep my knee in his kidneys so he would not struggle and he stayed quiet. He must have been thankful to have been out of the water at last and was in no fit state to get up and run.

I once again told him to call his mate over, to shout out to him for some help. About twenty yards in front of us along the hedge, the other one suddenly appeared in the moonlight with his gun pointing at me.

I didn't have a chance to move as he fired a shot, hitting me across the top of my knees, taking the skin and the material of my breeches away with it. Some of the shot had also hit me across the back of my hand.

The man turned and ran off.

I was bleeding quite heavily but the adrenalin and anger stopped me feeling too much of the pain and cold, allowing me to get on with taking my prisoner back to the house and calling the local police. It was a long cold, bloody walk back to the house.

I made use of this time during the walk back to home. I got so much information from him; he was telling me everything I asked. He was scared and freezing cold and the fact that his friend had shot me must have really worried him. He knew it had been a very bad move for his mate to have fired the gun at me. I told him they would be charged with attempted murder as I knew he could so easily have killed me right there and then. I could be laying there dead right now and they both would have run off and left me!

On the walk back he gave me names and addresses of all

known poachers in the area in his fear to cooperate with me. I just grilled him intensely until I got him inside the house and tied him to one of the dining chairs in the kitchen. He was still handcuffed behind his back and couldn't move when I woke Joan up to help me. I then called the police and asked them to go and collect his accomplice who had probably gone home, as well as sending someone to pick this one up.

I had given Joan my thick blackthorn truncheon which I kept hanging in the kitchen and told her to use it if he dared to move, as I had to leave them alone to see to my legs which were bleeding heavily and just starting to hurt and feel uncomfortable. I must have looked in a bit of a state with blood pouring out from my wounds; my trousers were covered in it. Joan was upset when she first saw me covered in blood. I was also very cold now and still soaking wet after my long walk back to the house.

The police arrived very quickly to arrest him for poaching and to interrogate him further. I had been able to give them the name and address on the phone when I got home of the one who had run away after shooting me, leaving his mate to take the blame. Police went straight to his home to arrest him, finding the gun as evidence as well.

Of course I had to give my statement of what happened after I had handed over my prisoner to the police. When they had arrived they had brought the police surgeon with them to deal with my gunshot wounds, having immediate medical attention and dressing my wounds.

Both men went to court and the one I caught in the river got a very heavy fine. The one who had fired the shot got three years for attempted murder. It was only sheer luck he had aimed low and not hit me in the chest.

Whilst I was asking the questions when he was sat in my

kitchen, I asked the poacher why he felt the need to poach pheasants on this estate. Why did he do it? His answer surprised me. He told me he had to get nine pheasants a night in order to pay off his fines to the court for poaching! Now what do you say to that?"

It was about three years later when he saw the same man who had been released from prison, having served his time. He was on his bike off out in the countryside. Dad said he pulled over in the Land Rover to talk to him and asked him where he was going. He was told he was going along to poach some salmon, just up the road off the edges of the estate, on the big river.

Dad said he had no ill feelings towards the man, giving him some cash to buy a drink to show he had no hard feelings after what had happened between them. At the same time the man also promised he would never come back onto the estate to poach again. As far as he knows he kept his promise.

Dad told me the poachers are so thick skinned and they are used to getting a good hiding, which they expect to happen, just as they would expect a good run at the sight of a keeper. What they don't always expect is that my father can outrun them even across ploughed fields and then wrestle with them when he's caught them, even though they may be much younger in years than he.

Another interesting incident occurred when it was daylight. Again in his own words:

"I had heard some banging as I was out feeding on the estate, thinking perhaps it was one of the other keepers having a shot. I drove my van over closer to the area where I had heard the shots being fired.

What I found were a couple of men with guns walking along the fields' edge a hundred yards ahead of me. I ran all the way up to within about ten yards away from them when one of them turned round and swinging his sixteen bore automatic shotgun at me shouting out "if you come any nearer I'll blow your guts out!"

So I stopped and just stood there fixed to the spot and told him "okay mate"

The sun happened to be shining and it shone down the end of his barrel as he pointed it at me. I could see the shining sunlight, as I knew it was an automatic and the breech was open letting light in, so hitting the cocking action where the cartridge would normally be. This meant the gun was unloaded. A bit of quick thinking and I decided I would go for him, now I knew his gun was unloaded. I think he realised what I had seen and he suddenly pulled a cartridge from his pocket and rammed it home into the barrel, pointing it at me again but only feet away this time. Now we both knew it was loaded.

I once again stood still in front of him; I knew he would shoot me as soon as look at me as by this time he looked very scared and nervous.

I told him once again "okay mate, you win, carry on."

This time I knew he could just blow me away, no doubt about it!

The two men turned away and ran off as fast as they could but the one who had pointed the gun at me kept turning round suspiciously to see if I was still there where he had left me. Maybe he thought I had backup on its way.

I watched to see what he would do and what direction he would take and melted into the background myself to watch him and his antics as he moved steadily forward out into the field.

He was heading into a field of thousand headed kale which grew to about two feet six inches tall, growing thickly. He suddenly ducked down to hide in it but I got his bearings. He must have thought he could see me from his position and look out to see if I would come back with some others. I did wonder if perhaps he wanted to go back the same way, where he had left me and was waiting for me to clear off.

I slunk off myself very quietly, once again melting back into the woods and under cover away from him. I knew what I had to do and how I was going to do it. I made my way back to the vehicle and had decided to go right round the top end of the field using the farm tracks in case he got up and went that way. I kept an eye open for him all the way round as I drove to the top of the huge field of kale parking up behind the hedge so he didn't see me as I got out. I got myself down amongst the kale moving forward to the position I had last seen him, creeping up as fast as I dare on him, as he still sat there waiting for who knows what.

It seems that he had been so busy watching and waiting to see which direction I might be going, he never heard or saw me as I crept up behind him in the kale putting my hand on his gun first to take it away from him in an instant. It had been lying beside him on the ground and I lifted it from him quickly as I put my knee into his back grabbing him before he could even make a move at me.

I meant to have him as he started to shout so I sorted him out quickly with a punch or two then removed the cartridges from his gun. I tied him up and hauled him up towards the vehicle, throwing him in the back.

It was only as I started to drive back towards home that the gravity of the situation suddenly hit me. This man had been still lying in wait for me in the field and he had purposely loaded his gun before pointing it at me, being ready to kill me in order to get away without a moments thought. I could have been lying out there dead in the field. He could have blown me away!

Anger welled up in me so strongly, I had to do something about it so I stopped the van and went round to the back, opening the door and gave him a good hiding reminding him why he was getting this, attempting to kill me. I was so angry, but I stopped myself and got back into the driving seat and pulled away again. Within a few hundred feet I had to stop once more as I felt the anger welling up inside me and repeated the thrashing over again as I couldn't get it out of my head what this man could have so easily done to me.

I must have given him at least four intense thrashings within the first mile before I got back to the house, to let the police deal with it all. He was screaming for me to stop in the end but I just didn't care. I was not proud of what I was doing but I knew enough about guns and firearms to know of the power they had. I had been at the wrong end of one too many times by now in my job. I felt he deserved what he got.

When the police arrived to collect him he went quietly, never uttering a word about what happened in the back of my vehicle. I don't think he could, given the circumstances, but at least I knew that I had dealt with him in my own way and felt all the better for it in giving my own punishment, which somehow made up for the injustice of it all. He was taken away and charged with attempted murder, but wasn't put away for what he did. I think he got all the justice from me on that day, rough justice, and he deserved all he got.

In one year at the Great Westwood estate I collected

twenty guns which had been taken from poachers. It was a perk of the job then. The police allowed us to confiscate them as they were caught in the act and if they were used in evidence they were given back after the trial as we often had more need for them, selling them on to people who would use them wisely. People knew if they wanted a gun that I nearly always had one for sale. I wouldn't sell them on to just anyone. They had to go to the right household and be used safely in the right hands. The poachers knew well not to ask for them back after they had committed the offences and none has ever done so right up to this day. They wouldn't have the cheek!"

KEEN TO MOVE ON

It was in July and August the plans would be made for the partridge shoots. The boss would have been in consultation with the head keeper to arrange the shoot days. They would have discussed the drives and where the guns would be standing. The boss would go out to the estate and together with the head keeper he would have a walk about to consider all the possibilities for a good days shooting, and notes would be made for the final plans.

The people who were to come and enjoy the shoots would have been contacted now, and money exchanged in readiness for a good days shooting as from the first of September. At the same time the partridge shoot dates will have been fixed along with the pheasant shooting dates.

Special guests would have been invited for each days shooting.

The head keeper would hold all the information and pass it on to the under keepers as and when it was necessary. He would have to make calls so as to provide loaders and picker uppers with the right amount of dogs to cover all the guns on each shooting day. Beaters will also have to be contacted and given dates so they knew when to attend. This sort of arrangements will often change throughout the late summer and early autumn and people will phone up to rearrange their own dates because of other commitments.

I remember the phone was always busy at this time of year and there were always a lot of people visiting the house who were connected to the shoot and estate.

During the summer months the tailors would have been contacted about this year's suits for all the keepers and visits to measure up would have been made to the tailors. A choice of the cloth, usually tweed would have been chosen by the boss and the head keeper in the right colours. They each got the same and the colour chosen would normally reflect the greens and browns of their environment. The tweed and colour was shown for the bosses' approval before being made up into the suits. Each of the men had a new suit for every season, as their boss always insisted they look smart on shoot days.

Lord Dudley had high standards and was proud of his workers portrayal as he was a public man himself and invited some very important guests as members of his shooting party. They had to have suits with waistcoats, white shirts and ties along with the appropriate hats. Boots with gaiters to keep their feet and ankles dry were essential. All trousers would be plus fours or knee breeches as was the custom for a keeper in those days. It made sense to dress properly and the boss never stinted on what was required to look the part. They would have an extra pair of trousers made as well for the normal job outside the shoot days as spare if it was needed.

Dad told me a tale about when the keepers all went for a fitting and measuring to the tailors. They always tried to go together on the same day. The Earl had his own good quality tailor who would measure each one of the men individually. One of the younger under keepers had taken the eye of the gentleman who was measuring him, leaving his hand lingering a little longer, touching and caressing him a little more than the others had been.

Dad said he made a bit of a fuss about this one young keeper and they all watched out when it was his turn to be measured to see how he would handle it and what he would do or say to him. The men liked a bit of a giggle and winked at him, possibly making him feel even more uncomfortable than he should have.

Doing the inside leg went well and when he was asked if he wanted a belt up the back the young man said *"not today thank you"* and darted out of the shop, head down, as quick as he could, leaving the others to follow, still smirking saying *"we have to catch a bus!"*

During the summer months dad recalls going along with the head keeper Bill Thornton to the dog show, Crufts, which was held at Olympia in London. Lord Dudley would send him to look out for new dogs entered in the working class show. Dad went along to accompany Bill as he was so good with the working dogs. A lot of the keepers would go along to the show to meet up as they were interested in looking for new breeders for their own dogs. It was a good social occasion for the keepers and those having connections with a working shoot that bred and sometimes showed off their breeds. They came from all over the country and it was a regular meeting place to catch up in the middle of the busy summer season and often a welcome break which was much needed by a keeper.

Lord Dudley would be away from his home as from the New Year right up until the weather improved in the late spring. Bill Thornton as head keeper would go to the big house to see his boss each morning he was there. He asked my father to accompany him at the request of Lord Dudley whom he seemed to get on well with.

Lord Dudley liked to be informed of the running of the shoot all throughout the spring and summer. He took great interest in what was being done as preparation to the autumn shoots. He wanted to know what was being repaired each day along with if there were any good shooting to be had and where it was to be. Sometimes it was pigeon or rabbits or if he could get in a few shots himself later that week once the partridges were ready and in season as of September.

When he came back to Britain after his time abroad from his second home, he would often have a film crew around the place filming. Because his family were well connected with actors and well known faces, many a time dad arrived on the scene at the big house for his ten-thirty appointments along with the head keeper to be confronted by a film crew. This was not unusual as often people like Peter Sellers, Gary Cooper and Cary Grant would be house guests and have some sort of filming taking place.

Dad said as he arrived one morning and came to the back door, he was approached by one of the film directors who introduced himself and asked if he may have a word with him when he was available. Dad told him he had an appointment with his Lordship at ten thirty and would see him after this.

Dutifully dad went on to see the boss to discuss the day's activities out on the estate and when he had finished he went to find the film crew and its director.

The man told my father he was looking for an actor to play the part of the game keeper in Lady Chatterley's'

Lover, in a new film adaptation he wanted to make. He told him he looked the part already, as he was dressed in his very fine suit comprising of knee breeches and long green socks along with matching green tweed waistcoat and Norfolk style jacket, white shirt and tie along with his deer stalker hat. Obviously he looked perfect for the part, a handsome, traditionally dressed game keeper.

Dad said he knew he looked smart in his everyday working clothes but on these occasions when he met the Earl in the morning he would always make more of an effort as his boss expected him to look like a good country gentleman in his presence.

The film director told him he would like him to try out for the part as he was a good looking man who fitted the role exactly. Dad told me he declined the offer on the day but he was flattered. However, more recently he said maybe he should have taken on the part as he could have made a bit of money and had some fun along the way.

He did also say he was in so much trouble with my mother at the time he could not have said yes, even if he had wanted to. He said he never told her about the film crew as he was too scared to at the time. I do believe he was having one or two women chasing him at the time as he was a good looking man, especially in that outfit. Mum was doing the right thing and keeping him on a short rein.

It was October and all were dressed up smartly and ready for the first shoot of the pheasant season. The keepers would all gather at the big house awaiting the appearance of the boss with his guest guns. They would come out to the vehicles and make their way towards the first drive of the morning.

Amongst the work party there would be pickers up; men with dogs, some who had been training the younger generation all summer to go and retrieve the birds as they fell to the ground after a successful shot.

The beaters would also have assembled there after having been contacted a day or two beforehand so they knew what was required of them on the day. Usually the younger ones would have been placed out earlier in the morning already by the keepers as "stops" on the prominent edges of the woods, to stop the birds wandering off down the hedgerows and across the fields. The young beaters would be instructed to make a few sharp tapping noises just enough to make the pheasants stay inside the wood and hitting the hedges in one small area to keep them there without scaring them too much.

On a partridge shooting day things were a little different. The birds would have to be walked up along the grassy hedgerows, flushing them out into the open ground. They would be hidden in the kale and thick undergrowth of the game crops all around the edges of the woodlands so a number of the dogs were used for this.

Most of the guns would bring along a companion or loader to help carry the guns and cartridges and some even brought along their own dogs for the day which helped in picking up close to their own stands.

When all were gathered and ready to leave from the meeting place, usually the boss's house, they would set off in a convoy of vehicles, usually Land Rovers, as these vehicles can cope with the terrain, whether it is mud, water or hills.

On arrival at the first drive of the day the head keeper

would help the boss in directing the guns to their peg positions, usually along the bottom of the woodlands and to each side of the adjoining fields.

The keepers along with the beaters would be positioned along the tops of woods hopefully having formed a straight line. Sometimes tapes of coloured plastic strips would have been put out early in the morning to stop the pheasants roaming onto the fields if the wood was to be shot that day. If the pheasants saw the coloured tapes it would scare them enough to keep them inside the wood but not enough to make them fly. This would have been done as the stops had been taken out early in the morning, from seven oclock and all would be set up in readiness. However at times it was only done as the under keepers and beaters got to the woods just before they were ready to start. A couple of the beaters in this case would quickly and quietly cut across the field to the woods, before the others got there to unravel the tape across the bottom of the wood well in front of where the guns will be standing at the end of the drive.

As the pheasants are flushed through by the beaters walking through the wood in a line, the pheasants see the tape ahead of them and most get up to fly at the sight of it, hopefully in a continuous stream. Of course some fly back and want to go home as they feel unsafe.

There is an art to making the pheasants fly. They always want to fly home and using this principal it is possible to steer the pheasants away from home so that they will try to fly high and turn back gaining height in order to do so. This makes for better shooting for the guns who will talk about a high pheasant for a long time afterwards whether they were able to hit it or not.

It is usually the head keeper who will blow his horn or whistle as a signal to the guns when they are ready to start the drive. It was often the case as it still is today that the guns will draw straws for the number of a peg. Each one will be numbered, say one to ten and the gun will have to stand on that number for each drive throughout the day. This is done usually before they get to the first drive of the morning

However, for very influential guests and those considered by the boss to be worthy of the very best chance of getting a few good choice shots, certain pegs will be handed out or marked slightly differently. These would always be in the ideal spot in the wood for those people, as the test of time in trial and error will have proved many times over the amount of birds that will normally fly over this position during a drive.

The guns are by now ready and waiting at their pegs along the ends and edges of the woods and will have already blown their own signal, usually by using a hunting horn but sometimes a whistle. This is the signal that they are ready to start, in response to the signal given by the head keeper. At the sounding of the horn from the guns, they are ready to fire their guns at will.

The beaters are now instructed to move forward in a line across the woods and sometimes out into the fields, hitting the undergrowth as they go to dislodge the hiding pheasants in the thickets and bushes. A pheasant isn't silly enough not to try and hide and sometimes is in very thick undergrowth. Dogs are used to push out those hiding underneath it all. This is often where a smaller child beater will come in very handy as they can get under where an adult can't. My brothers and sisters and

I have all done some beating during our younger years and I remember some very happy times out in the woods whilst beating and being asked to get into places where the men could not get into, to flush out the stray nervous pheasants when there haven't been any dogs available. Occasionally in some deep thickets a woodcock or two may be encouraged to fly along the line. These are much prized by the guns as they are very fast flyers and not the easiest bird to shoot. When they get up the beaters will often shout out to the waiting guns, *"woodcock, woodcock!"* to alert them that they are about.

For those guns out in the fields to the sides of the woods, they are not allowed to fire behind them as the pickers-up are usually there marking where the birds fall. Many a time the waiting guns will see the perfect shot of a rabbit coming out of the woods edge and out into the fields but have to ignore them as it is too unsafe unless it is a bird high in the air. There would be men with dogs waiting behind them often as not so they couldn't shoot wherever they liked as it would be too dangerous to do so.

As the beaters walk through the woods they are instructed to stop and start by the keepers depending on the way the birds are getting up and flying. The guns don't need to have a mass of birds getting up all at once as they can only fire a couple of cartridges at a time.

This is where loaders are very useful during these intense moments, as they often point out stray high birds that are on their way over to the guns positions, as well as loading both broken open barrels as soon as the gun is emptied into the air.

Loaders are very often the guns' own keepers from

their estates and those connected to shoots and will often be as keen and supportive in the ways of the shoot and the etiquette of the day. Many of the guns of those days were the gentry and royalty. Those who were asked to help out as loaders had to be of a certain background with quality and reliability, allowing the gun some privacy whilst talking to his companions along route to the next drive and out in the fields. They had to be able to keep a still tongue as well as knowing where to point out his next best shot if he hadn't already spotted it himself. They had an eye for it all themselves and it was no mean feat to accompany these gentlemen out on a days shooting.

The guns will often bring along a pair of guns so as to make the operation a little smoother and only need to exchange a gun each time a shot is to be fired. It can be a continuous exchange if the drive is good and there are plenty of birds going over. The loader is removing the spent cartridges and reloading passing over the gun as he accepts the other one in return. Sometimes they have a long time to wait for birds to fly over them. The wind direction is all important as to which way the birds will fly.

The beaters will be instructed to stop and stay silent at times if the birds are flushed out too quickly. The pheasants will run up to the tape ahead of the men, taking flight as they see the stretched out brightly coloured pieces of plastic flapping around in the distance. Some are braver and will go right up to it getting up at the last moment as the men appear behind them beating the bushes and making a lot of noise, then flying out over the waiting guns ahead.

Despite the way the birds have been pushed forward

they do have a chance to escape and many do so by staying on the ground and running across the fields and hedgerows at the sides of the wood if they get the opportunity. This is when the stops are considered useful as the pheasant will be cut off in its tracks by seeing a body there, usually waving a flag and hitting the hedge or fence with his stick making a noise. They can still refuse to fly and escape back behind the beaters to live for another day, which happens with many. Guns with pegs in the fields at the sides of the drive will have the opportunity to have a few decent shots at these fliers as they come past.

It is at this point, as the line of beaters passes the stops out along the hedgerows and in the fields that they are waved in and called to come and join the line along with the other beaters.

Some of these stops would have been out for hours sometimes in heavy rain, sleet or snow and usually since the sun came up. It is a long, cold wait, listening out for the guns firing around the estate all morning hoping they are going to come to the woods you are guarding. Some of the youngsters would get bored in their job, being only too ready to be called in to do something a bit different.

On a number of occasions when all the beaters have gone home at the end of the day, it was usually the mother who would phone up and ask where her son or daughter was, as they had not yet arrived home. In a quiet frenzy of panic it dawned on my father during the telephone conversation what had probably happened and where he or she was. Reassuring the mother that all was in fact well, and suggesting maybe he had stayed on to talk with some of the others afterwards or had been playing a game or two of darts in the beaters' shed; dad would jump in the jeep, going onto the estate to locate the errant beater. He said this happened on a number of occasions and on different estates he worked on. He would find them where he left them many hours before, they being too scared to move more than a few yards away in any direction. He had given them such a roasting when they had been placed there first thing that morning.

I know this myself as it had happened to me aged about nine once, but my adventure only lasted until the lunchtime and two drives later. He did come back for me as soon as he realised I wasn't there as he needed me for another drive straight after lunch. I soon learnt the drill and never got left behind again after that. It's compulsory; you have to do it once as a child of a gamekeeper.

I already knew as he recounted all this, how the youngster had been given such a talking to when he had left them, as I had undergone this initiation myself; his instructions just as the sun was coming up that morning was not to move from this spot until he called you in. It was done in such a tone of voice that you didn't argue with it, you knew he meant it. Very efficiently they had done their job, just as I had done before them, but as he had not called them himself towards the end of the drive, they had been too scared to move and dutifully stood at their posts. He must have made a very deep impression on us young beaters for us to have stayed where we were put.

Of course my father always made sure they got home and told them what a good job they had done that day and gave them a little extra to make up for being left out in the field for so long and to keep their silence perhaps.

He would also always drop them straight home to make up for what had happened. If they still turned up again next week he knew they were keen.

Back to the shooting, the gun dogs will be sent out to retrieve after each shot. The men with dogs will have been asked to stand a few yards behind the waiting guns so they can see where the birds fall. Occasionally the birds will run off after being hit by the guns and on landing, the dogs will give chase. Of course the bird will have been injured by the shot enough to drop it to the ground, but adrenalin must have tried to get it out of there as fast as it could. Rather than allow the bird to suffer in this way once it has been fired on, the dog will lift it after giving chase and take it back to its master where with a quick flick of the wrist its neck will be broken, if found still alive.

Usually as the beaters have walked through the wood and the tape is in sight, it is the end of the drive and a whistle is blown by the head keeper to signify no more shooting is to take place by the guns and they are to unload. A horn or whistle will also be blown within seconds from the guns to signify the end of all shooting on that drive.

Health and safety on a shoot day is vitally important and all the gentlemen who shoot will have all the rules and regulations thrown at them by their own fathers and mentors over the years before or they would not have been allowed out with a gun themselves on a shoot day.

It is very rare to have someone shoot low and towards the beaters but it has been known on the odd occasion on most shoots.

I can vouch for this myself as I felt the sharp sudden

onset of pain in my rear end, after the bang of a gun, having been caught on the edge of the spread of his shot, as I crouched in a slight ditch. I had been put there by my father just before the beginning of the drive as a stop not too far in front of him. I assumed he had seen me along with the others and knew not to fire in my direction whilst I was doing my job. Maybe his judgement was clouded by the cherry brandy he consumed during the lull of shooting or at his lunch break.

I can still remember the sting of it.

My dad told me he must have hit the trigger by mistake as he was lifting the gun. He had a few quiet words with the gentleman in question afterwards to point out how dangerously he had acted.

The shoot experience would consist of four to six drives taken over two halves of the day.

A break of about an hour would normally be taken sometimes in huts in the woods by the beaters or if close to the head keepers' cottage they would congregate in the game huts close to the house. There they would eat their sandwiches or soup which was sometimes laid on by the head keepers' wife. They had hot drinks and fruit cake also supplied on occasions.

Meanwhile the guns would often go along for a lunch at the boss's house.

They would all appear back on the shoot at the first drive of the afternoon, happy, complete and ready for the next bout.

My father reminds me on one of the morning drives about eleven thirty and just about to go into the third drive of the day he came out along the hedgerow himself to call in one of the young stops who was along the side of the wood. She had been left there early in the morning as is usual and been told to tap the tree and anything else which would make a bit of noise to keep the pheasants at bay in the wood. If she saw a pheasant coming towards her she was to tap like mad and frighten them enough for them to run the other way. Well, she did this and had worn a patch close to the trees' roots system. When my father came to collect her he saw that she was tapping on metal. On closer inspection he realised what she had been tapping on all morning, it was an unexploded bomb as well as the tree roots.

This bomb had all the fins still intact with its tail end sticking out between the tree roots. The roots had grown round it and they had grown and fanned out to balance it; it must have lifted the bomb closer to the surface.

She had disturbed all the soil around it exposing it more, unaware of what she had been tapping on for all those hours. He said her stick was well beaten where she had hit the metal as well as the tree. He enquired if she knew what it was and didn't say anything to her in case she got scared.

My dad took her away and went to find the boss to discuss whether to finish the day and call in the bomb squad or do it when they went for lunch.

They decided they would carry on for the last drive before lunch as they were far enough away to not be a danger. After all, the bomb will have been there for many years, only being exposed because of the trees natural growth where they spread to give more stability as they grow larger.

During the lunch break many trucks arrived from the bomb squad, detonating it where it lay. All the beaters heard the explosion as they were still eating their lunches. The blast could be heard quite loudly a couple of miles away. When the all clear was given by the soldier in charge, all the guns and beaters were allowed back onto the estate for the last drive of the day, so all was not lost. My father went along to inspect the damage which was close to one of his pens. The blast had apparently made a huge crater which they left as a memento of the occasion but no real harm was done otherwise.

During the shorter days of the winter when the afternoon sun was going down and they were running a little late for the organised drives of the day, they would elect to go and shoot a few ducks on the pools and ponds on the estate. If it was getting dark and the ducks were all in flight the beaters would be sent home except for the most experienced after the last drive. Beaters weren't needed the same at the pools except to stand in position over the fields just away from the ponds. They would help with the picking up along with the men with dogs.

The job didn't end there though for the keepers as they had to make a count of the day's total of birds shot, hanging them up in pairs usually a cock and a hen where possible. They had orders from the guns which had to be given to them by the boss after their lunch break. These orders for the game birds shot that day had to be taken up to the big house for his guests in readiness for them to take home when they left at the end of shooting. On the end of every drive the game would have been taken back to the game cart and strung up together and counted, so they knew how many were probably picked up and how many were still to be found. Most of the guns seem to know haw many they have shot and the loaders will tell the men with the dogs where to look. A simple record is kept and totalled up at the end of the day by someone who had been appointed to do the job. It was usually one of the under keepers.

Cards of the day's totals would have to be filled in and be ready to hand out to each guest gun of the days shoot as a reminder of the bag on that days outing.

As the beaters left for the day they would be paid for their days work and given a bottle of beer or cider as thanks for a job well done, to unwind with when they got home.

As for the guests, they would slowly depart as the late afternoon wore on after a chat with the boss and sometimes the keepers. It was a good day when the boss thanked all the under keepers as well as the head man. If they were lucky and everything had gone right with the day the keepers would occasionally be given tips by the happy guests for the good job done on that day.

My father after putting all the game away into the game larder went home to a good lamb stew and dumplings my mother had cooked for him. He said he always looked forward to this at the end of the day and it had become a bit of a tradition over the years. I know that after all the miles that are walked on a beat day that you are always ready for a good meal at the end of it leading on to a good long restful sleep that night.

The first days beating is not something that I would ever look forward to in the autumn because I was so unfit, but as the weeks wore on so did the stamina gain in strength. By the end of the season anyone who doubted their fitness will generally be in pretty good shape.

Beaters are expected to get over ditches and plough

through heavy muddy fields. Each step would get heavier as the soil stuck in thick wads to your boots as you crossed a ploughed field because the next drive would always be over that next ploughed field, you could bet on it.

Sometimes it would be a mile or two away and only your legs to get you there. If you were small you were expected to go under and through the thickets where the men were too tall to crawl into. Streams had to be crossed and if there were no bridges or even a plank of wood traversing the narrowest bit, you had to wade in after gauging the depth to know whether you would be getting a soaking that day.

On a warmer day you still had to be dressed for every eventuality and you got hot with a hat on, then if you were put as a stop in contrast you would have to keep jiggling about in your job in order to stay warm. Dad would never let you wander from your post and jumping up and down was sometimes the only option of keeping warm whilst guarding your post for any stray pheasants creeping up on you along the hedges.

Saying that, I have some very happy memories of being the only person out in the middle of nowhere watching the clouds go by and seeing the beautiful sunrises. I have seen some beautiful cloud formations, watched the rain clouds building and seen the first snow flakes of the year during these early mornings. The smaller birds in their natural habitats along the hedgerows is something that not many people see every day or even have the patience to stand and watch, as I had the opportunity to do in those days. I had to learn to like my own company and thoughts.

There was very little Saturday morning television for

me when it was the shooting season, although I envied my younger sisters their warm and cosy seats in front of the fire watching *"Tiswas"*.

On days throughout the shooting season the feeding and watering of the pheasants will continue all throughout the winter to keep them in or close to the woods

This needs to be done whatever the weather, morning and evening. It becomes a ritual act on getting up early in the morning even before the sun rises. Dad loves this time of the day and is often up even in the winter before six oclock. He says it is the early bird that catches the worm. He will do a couple of hours feeding before coming home for breakfast and then carrying on to do his other work of the day. It is often whilst he is out feeding when he spots the next most important job to be done for the day.

During the winter months for a keeper the days will revolve around the feeding and organising of the next shoot day which will occupy much of their time. On certain days the boss will need to be consulted over positions and thinking about the weather and wind direction and alternative ways of taking the drives to get the maximum shooting in for the guns on the day.

Many of the smaller estates only have one shoot a week throughout the autumn and winter months. The bigger ones will have two or even three or more each week as they have a lot of ground to cover and not so much disturbance to the pheasant and partridges out in the woods.

On the Great Westwood Estate the shooting finished at the end of December as his boss Lord Dudley went away usually straight after Christmas. He would go off to his second home in America and not return until the good weather was with us in Britain.

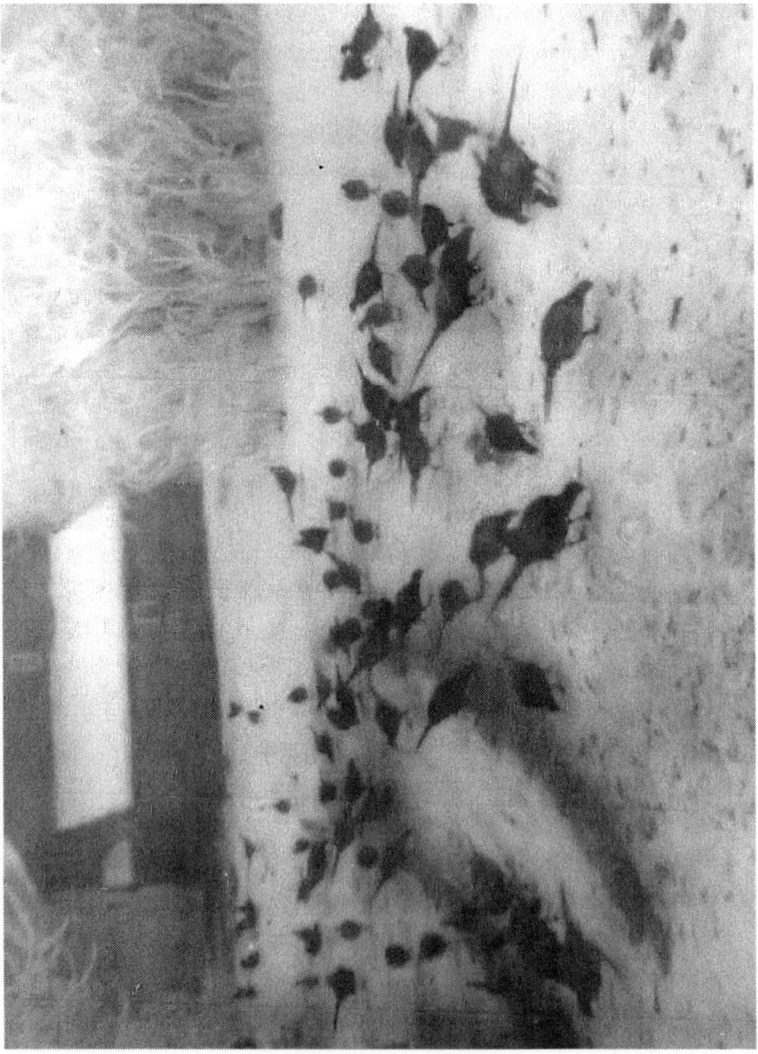

CHRISTMAS SPIRIT

In one of my conversations with my father he told me a funny story that happened to him at Christmas time.

It was usually a good time to take a brace of pheasants to the tenant farmers and those that had helped out on the estate. He would do this every week anyway after a shoot, if he knew they wanted some pheasants, instead of taking them to the game dealers and butchers. On the week they had shot before Christmas he would take some round as a small gesture that almost always went down well and many were grateful for it.

There was a nice and charming spinster who had a large house on the estate and she kept a number of cats. She would often have an order of a few rabbits as well as the pheasants so she could treat the cats as well as herself and her guests. She took in waifs and strays in the community and often the odd gypsy who would work casually on the farms about the estate.

Dad was shown around by her in the large house, seeing for himself how beautifully it had been decorated by a number of poor artists who had painted and decorated her home by way of thanks for her hospitality. She had done this ever since the war and had many guests over the years. She was a kindly lady of middle age and always loved to see my father of an afternoon, offering him a drink as they chatted.

She seemed a little lonely to him, as she would always try very hard to repay him with a meal or a very large drink, usually expensive brandy or whiskey of what seemed to him of gigantic proportions. He knew he didn't want any of it but felt bad about telling her that. She just wanted someone to stay and talk to her.

He also often declined a meal that she had nearly always cooked especially for him, saying that he had just eaten before he came out, whether he had or not. When he refused the meal she told him she had something on the stove and showed him into a beautifully decorated sitting room to wait and have his drink until she came back from the kitchen after a few minutes.

Whilst she was gone dad looked around him seeing all the decorations about the room and in particular the many Christmas cards festooned on strings along with the holly and mistletoe all around the fireplace. It was well done and obviously she had been sent many cards from friends and had taken plenty of time on dressing the room for her visitors with all this decoration. It was he said." *"The perfect Christmas picture with a beautiful huge log fire burning in the grate."*

He knew he was too polite in accepting this very generous glass of brandy and wished she had given him a smaller glass. He had tried to drain it but could only take small sips as he wasn't a drinker at all. In fact, he hates drink.

He had on other occasions when calling, managed to slip most of it into a plant pot or down the sink if he had been in the kitchen before he left.

On this occasion he could see nothing to pour it into, so without thinking he threw all the contents into the beautiful log fire with very dire consequences.

He told me he thought it would just sizzle away quietly.

But no, it whooshed and blew out like petrol, out into the room, taking in all the cards and holly and mistletoe surrounding the huge fireplace. The flames were up the walls licking the ceiling as he flapped around trying to think how to put it out and what to do next. He watched as he saw the rug ignite as well as the wall above the fires mantel-piece. He told me *"I was very scared!"*

He couldn't for the life of him think what to do next and it fleetingly went through his mind that it was perhaps a good time to call the fire brigade quite soon. He told me he really thought the flames were beyond him to put out and he was hoping she wouldn't come back in just yet.

Then it occurred to him that he had some explanations to make to this poor woman on how he had achieved the destruction of her beautiful sitting room and that she was bound to be quite angry with him.

He was at his wits end by the time he saw her enter the room, standing there quietly in the doorway, not uttering a word she looked on quietly transfixed by the scene that greeted her.

All dad could come out with as a satisfactory statement was, *"sorry, but a log fell out of the fire!"*

With that she stirred herself and seemed satisfied thankfully with his explanation and walked in to gather the remains together. They pulled all the stuff off the mantelpiece and the wall, throwing it all on to the fire where it continued to burn along with all the charred and blackened Christmas card remains in the grate. The entire wall around and above the fireplace, ceiling and mantelpiece were blackened and scorched along with the hearth rug. There were no longer any Christmas cards or indeed decorations or wallpaper left along that side of the room.

When he left there he was so thankful the flames had died down quickly, once the decorations had been removed and put into the fireplace. He was so ashamed of his behaviour and knew he could never tell her what had really happened with the brandy. He said she was such a kind and forgiving soul and he didn't want to hurt her feelings. He had done enough damage already. He must have ruined her Christmas anyway.

To make him feel even worse the poor woman had thrust a small bottle of brandy into his jacket pocket as he left telling him he had missed out on his drink and probably needed one after that episode when he got home for the shock. He said *"What can you say to that?"*

When he was first employed by Lord Dudley, dad was told by his boss that he wanted him to become head keeper eventually. This was a huge undertaking as the estate was so well managed by the current head keeper, having five under keepers to watch over, he felt not quite ready and up to it yet. Lord Dudley had seen in the first year there were far more partridges on his beat on a shooting day and a large amount of pheasants as well on his patch, so he knew how to keep them there.

He was asked by lord Dudley how was it he managed to have so many partridges on the bits of the estate that were in his care. He replied *"I've killed all the foxes in my beat and eliminated most of the predators and vermin."*

Dad said he wanted to learn more under the careful eye of the current head keeper, Bill Thornton, but Bill didn't want to stay on any longer. He had made a success of the shoot and was now ready to pass it on to another.

Dad told me Bill Thornton was a little afraid of Lord Dudley's shouts and wanted to leave as he was a bit too much for him to handle. He was worried by his bosses shouting which he did to a lot of his servants, whoever they were. He had secured a job to go to when he left in the March of 1960, going to Blandford St. Mary in Dorset, once again as a keeper.

My father was called up to the big house by the boss one day just short of two years after he joined the shoot as an under keeper and given the role of Head Keeper to the Great Westwood Estate. Along with the job went a house right in the heart of the estate. It was called Berry Bushes. He would continue with the four other keepers he had worked alongside, but now take the leading role and responsibilities that went with it.

It was time to move on up and take charge of the Earl of Dudleys' Great Westwood Estate.

This Man Is Holding The Great Maharaja Ranjit Singh's Butt

My father's life long friend Mr Ronald Wharton will be featured in my next book titled:

My Father
The Gamekeeper
Top Gun

In this book I will explain what this above statement is about.

Ron is one of the greatest master craftsman my father has ever known. He has on many occasions repaired my father's guns.

It is through Ron's work with rifles and shotguns and his own fascination with the countryside that they have remained such good friends.

Because of his excellent qualities as a friend, this man has been, and still is, held in such high esteem by my father and hence my father is still in desperate search to fulfil this mans order of 1968.

Dad has tried, and still is trying so hard to find him the Ferret Eggs he ordered so long ago. After all, one cannot disappoint such an immaculate craftsman who is also associated to the Great Maharaja of the Punjab in India.

Now affectionately known as Bunduki, Rigby Ron has through the years supplied the highest quality firearms to many people from all walks of life internationally, with the highest quality and friendly service.